LIVING WANDS OF THE DRUIDS

"As with all of Hughes's Druidic books, this one offers a unique insight into hereditary Welsh Druidism, which is distinctly different in beliefs, practice, and flavor from the more well-known international neo-Druidry. While this is very different indeed from most modern practices, and indeed some of the Irish traditions (e.g., the Irish Aspen funereal wand), it makes sense entirely as a means to harness the living and natural power of trees and shrubs for magical purposes. This book only covers ten trees, but it is very comprehensive and practical in terms of understanding the principles and techniques that could then easily be employed with other plant species. An excellent, instructive guide and a very worthwhile addition to any Druid's library."

LUKE EASTWOOD, AUTHOR OF *THE DRUID'S PRIMER* AND *THE DRUID GARDEN*

LIVING WANDS OF THE DRUIDS

HARVESTING, CRAFTING, AND CASTING WITH MAGICAL TOOLS

JON G. HUGHES

Destiny Books
Rochester, Vermont

Destiny Books
One Park Street
Rochester, Vermont 05767
www.DestinyBooks.com

Destiny Books is a division of Inner Traditions International

Cataloging-in-Publication Data for this title is available from the Library of Congress

ISBN 978-1-64411-803-0 (print)
ISBN 978-1-64411-804-7 (ebook)

Printed and bound in the United States by Lake Book Manufacturing, LLC

10 9 8 7 6 5 4 3 2 1

Text design and layout by Priscilla Harris Baker
This book was typeset in Garamond Premier Pro with Belda, Futura, Gill Sans, Legacy Sans, and Nelson used as display typefaces

To send correspondence to the author of this book, mail a first-class letter to the author c/o Inner Traditions • Bear & Company, One Park Street, Rochester, VT 05767, and we will forward the communication, or contact the author directly at **jongarstanhughes@gmail.com**.

Scan the QR code and save 25% at InnerTraditions.com. Browse over 2,000 titles on spirituality, the occult, ancient mysteries, new science, holistic health, and natural medicine.

For Anwen Maria Agatha Gallagher

CONTENTS

INTRODUCTION

In all its manifestations—from flamboyant stage magicians to ancient Egyptian pharaohs, from fictitious apprentice wizards to mystic shamans—the wand, in one form or another, is seen as *the* ubiquitous element of metaphysical workings and mystical power.

This iconic magical device appears in a bewildering array of forms, wielded by an even more bewildering array of characters. But whatever you may think of its image and reputation, it cannot be denied that the wand has found its own place in our popular culture and zeitgeist. Wiccans, witches, diviners, Druids, occultists, and other "workers of magic"—just about every metaphysical practitioner employs some form of wand in their workings.

Although most modern images of Druids show them holding a staff and using it as the chosen device for magical workings, the oral tradition of the Druids, and in particular the Welsh tradition, as we shall see, tells us something very different. While the staff does have a role to play (we shall also explore this in some detail later), it is the wand that holds pride of place as the foremost conduit for spiritual power throughout every aspect of Druidic lore.

The information and techniques explored in this book are essential to understanding how and why Druidic wands are so important and why they hold such a prominent position in the Druidic tradition.

In the following chapters we will focus on the use of wands and similar conduits within the practices of the ancient Druids, beginning at a time thousands of years before the Celtic influence arrived on the shores of Ireland, Wales, Scotland, and Cornwall and began calling the ancient learned pagan magic-workers by their Celtic name, *Druids*—a title they brought with them from Eastern Europe.

We will see that each Druidic wand has a particular function and is used in a specific manner. Because of this, each is crafted in a meticulous way in order to serve its purpose to the best effect. We shall explore each wand in detail, from simple rudimentary wands to the more complex and sophisticated compound wands, along with some of the more unusual and lesser-known arcane wands used by our Druid ancestors. First we must anticipate a question that is likely to arise while developing one's understanding of Druidic wand lore: How do Druidic wands differ from other wands, and what is it that defines their unique position within Druidic lore?

ONE

LIVING WANDS

Vital Spiritual Conduits of the Druids

The fundamental principle that underpins the effectiveness of all forms of wands, staffs, and other devices used within the Druidic tradition is that in order to channel the energies of the adept and influence those energies with the wand's own attributes, the wood from which the wand is crafted must be living when it is used. By *living* we mean that the wood must still contain the vital living sap of the tree from which it has been harvested so that this vital sap may impart the virtues and attributes of the chosen tree to the channeled energy of the adept, enhancing and elevating the adept's energy and intention as they pass through the heart of the wand.

This simple yet profound understanding of nature contradicts the beliefs of many, if not all, of the other wand-using traditions, both in their recorded history and in modern neo-pagan belief systems we may encounter today. Consequently, it begs the question: How do other belief systems explain how their wands and staffs work if they are using dead, inanimate wood to craft them?

I have posed this question to a large number of devotees from a wide range of belief systems and, with the odd exception, I have received one of two replies. The first and by far the most frequent response was that they had never really considered how their wands work, in the same way as they had never considered how any of their other ritual devices work. Their magical devices are simply there to fulfill their function and, as long as they do, how they function is not really important. The second most frequent reply, and the one that required further exploration, was that the material from which the wand is crafted does not need to be alive in order for it to be effective as its attributes are retained by the wood (or other material) until it decomposes. In fact, not only are the attributes locked into the dead wood, but they become more concentrated and powerful as the material matures and as the wand is used over and over again.

To some adepts this latter explanation may seem convincing and it does justify the use of other inanimate materials, such as metals, crystals, and others, as wands. But the Druidic tradition invests its power in our relationship with the energies of a living nature, and so I remain unconvinced of the use of inanimate, nonliving devices—in the same way as I fail to see the effectiveness of using store-bought dried herbs with undefined provenance in remedies and potions, or dried flowers in flower magic philters.

One of the main difficulties I have is with the repurposing of bits of abandoned or broken wooden furniture to craft wands. Having seen recovered chair legs being turned on an electric lathe in order to manufacture an intricately fashioned wand, I can only question the validity of such a magical device. I have the same misgivings about elaborately turned wands that are available for purchase as manufactured commodities on websites and in stores. How can such items be legitimately used by anyone other than as toys or decorative accessories?

Having said all that, I am the first to defend every individual's right to arrive at his or her own understanding of what is appropriate and what isn't, and I am not presenting my understanding as superior to or better than any other. I only suggest that living wands are much more harmonious with an understanding of natural magic and the vitality of a wholesome, living, and natural world.

With this in mind, the first step in our exploration is to arrive at an understanding of what a wand is and why we choose to use it.

WHAT IS A WAND?

In searching for an answer to the question of what a wand is we turn to nature, as with all things in relation to Druidic lore.

Over the millennia we have discovered many (though by no means all) of the incredible qualities of nature and how, by working in harmony within this rich diversity of energies, we can create a synergy that we may utilize to our benefit in so many ways.

Druidic lore, at its very core, is harmonious with all of the natural world and it is undoubtedly the case that our Druidic ancestors would have spent their entire lives living *within* nature and working to understand all they could about the environment that guided their world and every aspect of their lives. They developed a uniquely intimate understanding of the forces and energies that controlled their existence—the forces of nature, the seasons, and the weather, together with all of the other natural gifts that surrounded them.

In my homeland of Wales, then as now, one of the principal foci of the Druidic tradition has been the complexities of the indigenous botanicals, the trees and plants, that form the basis of the many potions, elixirs, and other tools of the Druids. I would suspect that for most readers, their main association with the image of the Druid, second only to the well-established relationship between Druids and our many stone circles, would be the inseparable relationship between Druids and trees. It is fair to suggest that the profound connection between the Druidic tradition and trees is stronger than that between trees and any other esoteric tradition. It is from this intimate relationship that we can begin to explain the meaning and purpose of the living wand in Druidic lore.

While there is no way of knowing for certain, it is reasonable to assume that the Druids' insight into the virtues and energies of the trees that surrounded them began at an early stage of Druidic tradition. We can make this assumption because much of the lore that has survived in the oral tradition of the Druids is founded in the understanding of trees and other botanicals. We are told that tree lore in particular formed a part of the early history of Druidic tradition and that trees contributed to many aspects of the everyday life of our Druidic ancestors by providing building material, fuel, tools, food, and many other necessities for survival. An understanding of the life-cycles, attributes, and virtues of trees was therefore essential from the very beginning.

Unlike today's society, in which we are concerned primarily with the physical and scientific aspects of what we can take from nature, our predecessors concerned themselves with both the physical and spiritual aspects of nature's gifts in equal measure. With the nature of trees being of particular interest, it is not difficult to understand why the oral tradition is full of so many detailed references to tree lore. Foremost among these is the tradition of the living wand.

The tradition teaches us that the living wand is "the vital spiritual conduit of the Druid." Critical to the understanding of the significance of this statement is a knowledge of the purpose and function of the living wand of the Druid.

PURPOSE AND FUNCTION

In its simplest form, a wand is a physical means of focusing, channeling, and directing the adept's intention. In doing so, the wand adds its own attributes and virtues to the intention, enhancing it with its characteristics as it simultaneously amplifies the intention and focuses it upon its intended objective. The word *intention* is used here to express the intended outcome of the adept's magical working and may be broadly compared to the more familiar word *spell*, which does not appear in the Druidic vocabulary. We will discuss intentions throughout this book, and in particular detail in chapter seven, "Using Your Wand." The Druid uses a wand to project his will, focusing it toward its intended recipient or target. This, of course, may be done without the use of a wand and we see many instances of Druids casting their intentions by simply using their hand as a projection point. In using a carefully selected wand, however, the adept may further enhance his intention by adding the attributes of the chosen wood(s) and/or other botanicals in the wand to his own spiritual energies. In order to fully understand how this is achieved we must first consider the Druidic understanding of the physical and spiritual components that make up every *living* thing. In this instance I emphasize the word *living* and will go on to explain its meaning as it relates to wand lore.

Druids Do Not Worship

There is a further nuance to consider when observing the unique nature of Druidic intentions. Within Druidic lore there is no direct equivalent for the act of worship as it is understood in other belief systems—meaning the Druid does not *worship* nature per se. This is a consequence of the fundamental Druidic belief that there is/are no god(s) controlling our cosmos, our lives, or our destinies. Worship may be defined as the feeling or expression of reverence and adoration for a deity. As Druids hold the belief that there are no deities, then they have no place for worship in their rituals. Instead, Druids choose to invoke the assistance of nature—as a whole and in its individual manifestations—to help cast their intentions.

Worship, in the context of mainstream religions, for example, can be a means of repeatedly expressing adoration of a deity, typically frequently and over a long period of time. More often than not, this involves reciting the same standard prayer in exactly the same manner over and over again. In this context, we can see why there would be a need for a collection of standardized, often rhyming prayers, composed to be easy to remember. Conversely, as each Druidic intention is composed in response to a specific set of circumstances and as a means of directly communicating with nature or with specific living entities on a spiritual basis, we see that there is no need for standard verbal expressions for these intentions. It is highly unlikely that the same circumstances will ever repeat, and there are no gods or deities to which regular, repetitive prayers need to be spoken.

Cardinal Essences

Within Druidic lore each living entity is made up of three interdependent components, also called its *cardinal essences*: the physical manifestation of the entity, its portion of the communal energy or world spirit, and its own unique personal energy or spirit.

The entity's physical manifestation is its material existence in the mundane world. It is what we observe, what we touch, and what we taste and smell in regard to the entity. It is what we perceive as the entity's existence in fixed space and time.

The same entity's communal spirit is its portion of a worldwide energy that permeates all things in our universe. It is what makes the entity part of our worldly experience and the energy that all things living and inanimate have in common. Often referred to as *world spirit,* communal spirit is an element of many belief systems all around our planet. It is this communal energy that allows us to interact with and benefit from all other entities in our world, both on a spiritual and a material level.

Finally, the entity's personal energy or spirit is what makes each entity unique in its own right. This is what makes a single daisy flower different from all the other flowers in the world and identifies it as a unique individual, distinguished from all the other daisies that may surround it.

Each of these three components is obtained at the moment of the entity's conception or germination. The entity's physical manifestation is inherited from its parents and begins to decay when the other energies leave at the final moment of its existence. The entity's communal energy is what gives it life and it remains as the entity's life force until the entity's life comes to an end. At this moment it returns to the communal or world spirit and becomes a part of the whole once more. The entity's personal energy informs the behavior and attitudes of the entity for its lifetime. When the entity's life ends, the personal spirit dissipates, never to exist in the same form again, making it the only aspect of the entity's unique existence that may not be considered as "recyclable." While the physical manifestation decomposes and reenters the natural life cycle and the communal spirit returns to the ubiquitous world spirit, only the personal spirit dissipates, never to exist again.

Within this cycle we can see that as the greater part of our material and spiritual existence returns to a metaphorical pool of material and spiritual resources, a pool from which other living entities may draw their essential components, each of us has an individual and collective responsibility to live a life without contaminating the forces of nature that we temporarily possess. No matter how small this contamination may be, it will still influence the whole in a positive or negative way. And it is essential to consider the physical, communal, and personal energies in the materials, like wood, that make up our magical devices, such as wands.

Caring for Our Communal Spirit

Here is a simple example. Let's compare obtaining our individual portion of the communal energy, our small share of the world spirit, with removing a glass of seawater from an enormous ocean. While we have our metaphorical glass of seawater we are responsible for keeping it clean and wholesome. The choice is ours; we can simply keep it as we gathered it, we may seek to improve its purity, or we may choose to pollute it in some way. When the time comes to return the seawater to the ocean the choices we have made will have an effect upon the whole, no matter how small it may be. If, for example, we chose to dye the glass of water red, then this will have a small but nonetheless profound effect upon the entire ocean. This may well be an oversimplified example that does not survive much scrutiny, but nonetheless it illustrates our overwhelming responsibility as individuals and as a community to live wholesome lives and respect the natural world that allows us to do so.

For each of these spiritual energies, or cardinal essences, to be present in a wand and have an influence upon the intention being cast, the wooden wand must still contain its vital life energies, which we find in the wood and sap of a newly harvested piece of wood. As the harvested wood ages and its vital energies dissipate, it can no longer contribute its attributes and virtues to the casting, and therefore it becomes moribund and ineffective. This is why, within the Druidic tradition, only newly harvested living wands are used, while aged, seasoned wands have no place other than as decorative artifacts.

Spiritual Conduit

To recap, the primary function of any wand is as a spiritual conduit. It is a means of focusing, amplifying, and directing an intention toward its recipient, be it a person or an object. In using living wands, we imbue the intention with the virtues and attributes of the wood we chose to craft the wand from.

To accomplish this, focus the intention to the heel of the hand and then bring the wand's heartwood and sap into direct contact with that same spot before projecting the intention through the wand and casting it toward the intended recipient. In its usage, the wand may be compared to an electric conductor or electric cable, where the core conductive material (the metal wire inside the cable) is brought into contact with the energy source (the electricity supply) and conducts the energy directly to its intended recipient (be it an electric kettle, a desktop computer, or any other electrical appliance). In choosing the wood from which to craft a wand the adept considers the wood with the most appropriate attributes for the working he intends to undertake. (Similarly, the designer of an electrical cable may choose the most effective/conductive metal wire to use.)

Enhancing the Intention

Different woods enhance the projected intention in different ways. Careful selection and correct harvesting are important in crafting a wand so that the attributes of the specific wood can be absorbed by the intention as it passes through the wand. We will see in the sections that follow that various woods may be intertwined to form compound wands, in which the attributes of each wood combine in a way that allows for infinite variations of the comingled influences. In other words, each living wand may be specifically tailored to suit the intended use.

In some cases, a particular botanical, such as ivy, mistletoe, or honeysuckle, may be bound around the central wand in order to induce the effect of its attributes upon the final intention. In a similar way, when using staffs, a variety of adornments may be attached to the staff in order to imbue the staff's intention with their individual attributes. These adornments may include combinations of herbs, flowers, root-pouches, and the like, each of which will contribute their own natural attributes and add to those of the living wood of the staff itself.

Amplifying the Energy

In addition to enhancing the attributes of an intention, the use of a living wand may amplify the spiritual energy of the intention. In channeling the spiritual energy of the intention through the living sap and heartwood of the wand this energy is amplified by the living, vital energies of the wood. As we have discussed previously, every living manifestation of nature is imbued with its own vital spiritual energies—physical, communal, and personal. Passing an intention through a living wand and bringing it into contact with the wood's own energies amplifies the original spiritual energy of the intention, boosting it as it is cast. This process will become very apparent when we look at the ways and means of utilizing a living wand to cast an intention, for example in chapter seven, "Using Your Wand."

TWO

WOOD LORE

Donor Trees and Harvesting

In order to fully understand the nature of living wands and their application, it is essential to first understand the nature of the trees that surround us.

Trees form a fundamental part of Druidic tradition and arguably the core of all Druidic beliefs. So much so that many Celtic scholars suggest that the word *Druid* itself finds its origin in the lore of the tree. In the theoretical proto-Celtic language, the name may be rendered as *Dru-wid-s,* meaning "oak-knower" or "oak-seer." In ancient Welsh, we have the word *Dryw,* meaning "seer," while in Old Irish we have *Drui,* which translates as "Druid," "magician," or "sorcerer." Even more definitively, the Roman philosopher Pliny the Elder (23–79 CE)— author of *Naturalis Historia* (*Natural History*), considered the first true encyclopedia—considers the word *Druid* to have its root in the Greek word *Drys,* meaning "oak tree." The most general correspondence for the word *Druid* is "having the knowledge of trees (oaks)." It is worth considering here that "having the knowledge of trees" incorporates two meanings: knowing about trees and their characteristics and sharing the knowledge that the trees have.

We have discussed previously that trees, like all living entities, have three essential components: their physical manifestation, their portion of the communal or world energy (sometimes referred to as the world spirit), and their personal energy. In creating a living wand, the adept aspires to utilize all three essential components. Importantly, the adept attempts to match the tree's attributes and virtues contained within these three essential components to the intention she plans to cast. Light, delicate intentions demand the use of trees with delicate virtues, while powerful, forceful intentions require wood from a tree with powerful, strong attributes. By matching the tree's attributes to the proposed intention, the living wood's characteristics amplify the energy of the intention in a positive way, casting the most potent intention possible.

Each tree's intrinsic attributes and virtues remain consistent within its species, but they may be affected in a positive or negative way by a number of external and internal influences. Externally, a tree's attributes may depend upon its location, the general terroir (or environment in which it grows), and the influence of the plants that surround it or, in some cases, grow upon it. Other external influences include the method of harvesting, the season and time of harvesting, and how the harvested tree part is handled following its collection. Internal aspects affecting a tree's attributes include the age of the donor tree in relation to its lifecycle, its seasonal growth and vitality, and how soon after harvesting the living wood is crafted and used.

In addition to considering the appropriateness of the donor tree for crafting a particular living wand, we must also consider the physical and spiritual structure of the individual branch we intend to harvest and use. To do this it will be useful to first look at the various life stages and component parts of the tree itself. Within the Druidic tradition of Wales, the tree is an important resource at all stages of its lifecycle. In the same way, each component part of the tree is utilized in some form or another. We see that seeds, flowers, leaves, roots, bark, and branches all fulfill an essential role, as do seedlings, saplings, mature trees, and ancient trees. Each life stage and component has its own characteristics that provide benefits in a variety of different ways. Because Druidic lore only uses living botanicals, it is important to also take into account seasonal growth and seasonal reproductive patterns.

THE PHYSICAL STRUCTURE
OF A BRANCH

In a physical sense, a tree branch has the same structure as the tree's much larger trunk. Both a tree branch and a tree trunk are comprised of a central core surrounded by layers of heartwood that are themselves encased in older layers of wood with sturdy bark as an outermost protective layer.

Cross section of a harvested thorn branch to be crafted into a living wand, clearly showing the bark, inner wood, and sap core.

This stable, consistent structure common to all tree branches allows us to create a living wand from a chosen branch that both channels and amplifies the adept's intention while elevating it by adding the influence of its own virtues. The living, vital energy of the tree, which contains the virtues of its specific species, is contained in every component of the tree but is distributed within the tree by its living sap. This living sap reaches every extremity and component of the tree—its branches, leaves, flowers, seeds, and nuts. Tree sap contains nutrients and minerals and can be thought of as the "blood" of a tree. It rises from the roots deep in the earth, is influenced by the sun's energies as it does so, and is absorbed into every aspect of the tree as it travels through the trunk and branches.

When a branch is harvested with the intention of crafting a living wand, it contains the vital sap and energies of its donor tree. Crafting in the correct way will allow these virtues and attributes to be absorbed by the intention when it is cast. It is therefore imperative to craft and use the wand while the living sap is still present and spiritually alive, as it is this vital living sap that contains the spiritual energies of the tree. Without this vital living element, the wand is simply a piece of dead wood and serves no purpose whatsoever.

These concepts relate to our discussion of the cardinal essences. Like all entities, every tree, and subsequently every branch, has a unique physical manifestation that we may also call its physical appearance. Although each tree species may share certain physical characteristics, every individual tree develops its own unique physical appearance. Furthermore, no two branches on a single tree appear the same. These differences among individual trees and individual branches depend upon a wide range of influences that include weather, soil, location, surrounding plants, parasitic growth, inhabitation by insects and other animals, and more, the effects of which all shape the features of a tree as it grows.

THE METAPHYSICAL STRUCTURE
OF A WAND

In addition to the physical manifestation of the tree (one of its three cardinal essences), the tree is imbued with its own unique spiritual energies in the form of its remaining two cardinal essences: communal spirit and personal spirit. These spiritual energies enter the tree at the point when the tree begins its life and remain until it dies and decomposes. These two remaining cardinal essences make up the metaphysical attributes and virtues of the tree—not only the general attributes of the species of tree, i.e. the attributes of the oak, birch, or elm tree as different species with differing attributes, but also the attributes of the *individual* tree. Individual oaks, for example, will be imbued with different spiritual attributes absorbed from their growing environments, giving each separate tree its own unique spiritual signature. A tree's spiritual attributes are the principal attributes that the intention will absorb as it is cast. If the wood for the wand is chosen correctly, these spiritual energies will both amplify and enhance the intention's effectiveness by adding their own powerful influences.

In the same way that a tree's physical manifestation (its first cardinal essence) depends upon external influences, the spiritual energies of a tree are also influenced not only by the inherent variations among species, but also by the external influences absorbed from the tree's growing environment. No two trees, whether they are of the same species or not, have the same spiritual energies because each is affected by its unique growth factors. The differences in the spiritual energies of different types of trees, and among different individual trees, are important to consider when deciding which tree to select for a living wand; the chosen tree must have attributes sympathetic to the purpose for which the living wand is to be used. We will explore this in much more detail later in this chapter and in chapter three, "Wood Types."

First we will explore further the external influences that affect the spiritual attributes of a tree or branch, and how they affect the overall intention that a living wand casts.

CHOOSING THE DONOR TREE

Before we look in detail at the individual aspects that influence the spiritual energies of a specific tree, it is worth looking at the broad principles that inform the eventual properties of each tree as it grows. As discussed, each plant—be it a tree, flower, herb, or other botanical—is imbued with its own unique physical and spiritual properties. While it may be easy to see how a plant's physical characteristics are influenced by its surroundings, it is more difficult to understand how its spiritual attributes may be affected in the same way. For example, we may see how a tree twists and turns as it grows in order to fit itself into the most torturous situation—bending around rocks and finding its own space in the densest of forests. Here we see the natural ability of the plant to adapt to its environment and how profoundly its environment affects its physical growth. But we must also be aware of how its immediate environment affects its spiritual growth and development, and how its location influences its inherent spiritual properties.

Assessing Surrounding Influences

When we see a mature oak tree bound in ivy, it becomes clear that such a parasitic plant must have an influence upon its host, not only drawing its physical properties from the body of the tree but also impacting its spiritual attributes. When we see a rowan tree surrounded by ground-dwelling herbs, with the roots of both plants intertwined beneath the soil, it is easy to understand how each plant has an influence upon the other, both physically and spiritually. In the same way, when woodland trees grow in close proximity to each other, with their roots and canopies mingling together, we have to accept that each tree has a profound impact upon its neighbors. It is essential that we take these external influences into account when we consider each donor tree, and in particular we must take into account the influences that adjacent plants may have upon the chosen donor itself. In doing so, we see that some external influences complement a donor tree's attributes and amplify its characteristics, while others will contradict the donor tree's characteristics and dilute or even completely negate its spiritual attributes. Each potential donor tree will be affected by unique external influences; the adept must carefully consider each influence in order to choose the donor tree that best suits its intended application.

By far the majority of trees in the wild grow in groups of various sizes. This phenomenon results from the tree's natural method of distributing its seeds and the suitability of its surrounding environment. There are few locations that generate a more overwhelming connection with the spiritual world than the heart of a noble forest, a singularity that has been known according to Druidic lore from time immemorial. Few other belief systems have a closer connection to trees and forests than that of the Druids. We know that the original ancient gathering places of the Druids were the sacred forest groves where they conducted ritual and magic (see photo on the following page). This tradition continues to the present day when—along with the well-known stone circles—trees, forests, and sacred groves remain the focal points of the Druidic tradition.

The forests of Western Europe contain a wide variety of tree species but frequently are dominated by a specific type. Though many of the ancient oak forests were devastated as a result of the desperate need for the oak wood used to create the mighty naval ships of past eras, we still see oak forests, which are dominated by long-lived major oaks that give protection to younger oak generations. In similar ways, we see hazel forests, pine forests, and forests of every indigenous species. Many forests and woodlands contain mixed species, while some less numerous forests are made up of more unusual species, such as yew, which in most natural settings tends to grow as solitary trees or in small copses.

When searching for a donor tree, we most often find ourselves looking in a forest of mixed species. In this situation it is best to seek out a group of trees of the targeted species that are growing closely together. This way there is a better chance that each of the trees in the group will reinforce the spiritual attributes of its neighbors, thereby amplifying the desired attributes.

In other circumstances, it may be beneficial to seek out a specific tree of the chosen species that is surrounded by other botanicals that complement its attributes.

Grove with central working stone next to the stream at Lord Brandon's cottage, Killarney, Ireland.

In all cases, it is imperative that you do not choose a donor tree if it is surrounded by other trees or botanicals with spiritual attributes that contradict or negate the donor tree's principal attributes. It is interesting to note that in ancient man-made environments, such as the numerous "physic gardens" containing medicinal herbs and plants that we find in the monasteries and noble houses of our ancestors, trees and other botanicals were planted with consideration of these principles of external influence. Great care was taken to ensure that neighboring trees and botanicals did not contradict the properties of those planted around them. At the same time, other trees and botanicals were deliberately planted next to each other so that they would complement each other's characteristics—this widespread practice is called *companion planting*.

Location Factors

Other aspects that influence the attributes of a proposed donor tree are the specific location in which it is growing and in particular the nature of the soil, prevailing weather conditions, humidity, exposure, and other features of what may be called its terroir. We see among the mountains, valleys, and lakes of the Druidic heartlands of Ireland, Wales, Scotland, Southern Britain, and Northern France, for example, that forests and trees display a natural pattern of growth that reflects their individual reactions to their growing environments. Each hill or mountain has a unique boundary above which no tree can grow. This *tree line,* as it may be called, is defined by the difference in the environmental factors above and below it. Below the tree line the growing conditions are conducive to the growth and reproduction of the tree species we find there. Above the tree line, the growing environment may be too cold or too wet to sustain the growth of trees. It may be that the conditions above the tree line make the soil too unstable, or that the soil depth is too shallow, or perhaps the general area is too stony due to erosion. This natural selection phenomenon may be seen in other locations as well, such as sea cliffs and others, where the environmental factors are not conducive to tree growth. Other botanicals that have adapted to the conditions, however, may thrive there.

Environmental factors influence the growth and vitality of any potential donor tree. They can reduce or amplify the potency of its spiritual attributes, its vitality (the energies it contains), and its physical strength. Trees growing at the borders of their ability to exist, therefore, should not be selected as donor trees for two reasons. The first reason is that their spiritual vitality is compromised. The second reason is that they need to maintain their integrity to continue their struggle to survive and we must not jeopardize this by harvesting any of their physical or spiritual assets.

In conclusion, the adept must carefully consider all the aspects described above before selecting an individual donor for her wand. If chosen with care and intelligence, a donor branch may not only be imbued with the natural attributes and characteristics of the tree from which it is harvested but may also have its attributes enhanced and amplified by the influences of the trees and botanicals that surround it. We will explore the specific attributes of certain trees and other botanical species in more detail in the later chapters of this book.

SELECTING A DONOR BRANCH

When an appropriate tree has been identified, the next consideration is locating a suitable branch from which to craft the living wand. At first glance it may well appear that every tree grows its branches in a random, haphazard fashion, pushing out branches in every direction with no overall purpose. The function of a tree's branches, of course, is to seek sunlight, thereby allowing the tree's leaves to absorb the sunlight in order to sustain the tree's process of photosynthesis—converting light into energy to empower the tree's growth and reproduction. In seeking this life-giving light, some trees spread their branches in wide canopies and bask in the open spaces they find while others thrust their growth upward in an attempt to rise above competing trees and expose themselves to maximum sunlight. In some cases this purposeful growth is very obvious. For the majority of trees seeking light is a lifelong challenge that follows the seasonal cycle of the year.

This inherent principle of tree growth is important as it demonstrates the unbreakable link between trees and sunlight and the symbiotic relationship of sun and tree. The sun provides life-giving light for the tree and the tree acts as a carbon sink, maintaining the balance of our atmosphere. This relationship becomes important when the adept is seeking a suitable branch from which to fashion her wand. The physical aspects of the sun's influence may be summarized in two fundamental considerations: the orientation of the branch in relation to the main trunk of the tree and the orientation of the branch in relation to the progress of the sun across the sky. We will consider the spiritual aspects of these considerations in the next section.

Orientation

Each tree will grow its principal branches, those emanating directly from its trunk, in every possible direction in order to maximize the opportunities for reaching open space and sunlight. Those principal branches that succeed thrive, while those that don't die away. The successful branches sprout secondary branches with the same purpose, those secondary branches generate tertiary branches, and so on until the tree's canopy becomes fully developed. Though all these groups of branches may appear to generate randomly, only the successful ones survive, as in all processes of natural selection.

We have seen above that in crafting a living wand it is imperative that we retain the vital life-giving sap within the harvested branch, as it is this sap that contains the spiritual energies inherent in the tree. Every spring, this sap flows from the roots of the tree up through the trunk to the smallest branches, giving the tree the energy it needs for new growth. To maximize the amount of sap in a harvested branch, look for one that is directly connected to the trunk, not one at the end of a series of forks or divisions. While the tree's processes effectively counteract the universal force of gravity, sap, like most liquids, will still tend to travel along the easiest route available to it.

In addition to the position of a branch relative to the tree trunk, the adept should consider the orientation of a branch relative to the rising and setting of the sun. The movement of the sun in the sky imbues the living wand; it has relevance to where the wand has been grown and is to be used as well as the season and time when it was harvested and crafted. These connections reinforce the principle that each and every living wand is harvested and crafted for a specifically identified purpose and must be used while it is freshly harvested, still rich in sap and with a direct link to the time and place where it originated.

Much of the lives of the ancient Druids and their communities revolved around the progress of the sun across the sky. Through lengthy and detailed observation they recorded the exact point on the horizon where the sun rose and set, not only on the equinoxes and solstices but also on other auspicious days. We can still see the uncanny accuracy of their observations in the arrangement of the stone circles that decorate our landscape, each aligned within a few degrees of each other and each pinpointing a point on the landscape and the alignment of their stones with the sunrise or sunset on their appointed day. These detailed observations by the ancient Druids must have been done on a daily basis over a period of years in order to confirm their accuracy. Prototype wooden circles have been discovered that appear to have been erected in order to test their theories before they committed to the massive task of erecting the stone circles themselves.

Today we can define the point on the horizon at which the sun will rise on any particular day of the year, at any location, with the use of astronomical tables and a simple compass. Instructions to achieve this may be found in local libraries or by searching online resources. The important point is that in order to maximize the influence of a living wand on an intention it is imperative that the adept identify the rising or setting point of the sun on the horizon in relationship to the donor tree at the time when the living wand is selected to be harvested. The goal is to seek a branch to craft the wand that is aligned with the rising or setting point. This maximizes the sun's effect upon the spiritual energies within the branch.

We can see from the principles discussed in this section that each and every living wand must be identified and harvested for a specific purpose and at a specific date, time, and location in order to affirm its potency, relevance, and effectiveness. These principles further reinforce the understanding of why each living wand must be utilized as soon as possible following its harvesting and crafting, as it has no power or relevance once the sap has dissipated and the appointed time for its use has passed.

The Moon and the Sun

In the previous section we have explored the importance of the role of the sun in identifying an appropriate branch from which to craft a living wand. We must now also consider the spiritual influence that the sun and the moon have upon the living wand in relation to exactly *when* the branch is harvested and the effect this has upon its spiritual potency.

The sun, as well as the moon, had a huge influence upon the ancient Druids, on their lives and those of the communities they served. We understand from their oral tradition that the majority of their ritual and workings were (and still are) defined by the procession of the sun across the sky as well as the phases of the moon as it waxes and wanes. Many spiritual traditions place emphasis upon the times of change as the moon grows and diminishes and as the Earth experiences the equinoxes and solstices. In addition, we must not underestimate the importance of the sunrise and sunset, or the moments the moon rises and sets—in other words the points of change between daylight (day) and moonlight (night).

Put simply, branches harvested for living wands during daylight have a vital, powerful energy, amplifying the natural attributes of the potential wand. The same branch harvested beneath moonlight will have a more gentle, empathetic energy, magnifying the more subtle virtues of the chosen wood. For these reasons it is believed that wands harvested in daylight are more sympathetic to being used by a male, while those harvested by moonlight are more sympathetic to being used by females. Moreover, it is believed that branches harvested when the sun is at its greatest height carry the tree's most powerful daylight attributes, while those harvested when the moon is at its fullest maintain the tree's most potent moonlight virtues.

The Seasons

All trees, be they evergreen or deciduous, change their metabolism in response to the progressing seasons. Spring is the time for new growth, summer is the season of maturity, autumn is the time of fruitfulness, and winter is the season of dormancy. In most cases it is easy to see the tree's physical response to the changing seasons, but it is more difficult to understand the variations in the tree's spiritual attributes as it reacts to the changing seasons.

In spring, trees' spiritual energies are at their most vital and energetic. Their energies are growing by the day, and even young trees that lack maturity may make up for this deficit with their powerful, burgeoning raw energy. This dynamic is ideal for crafting wands that can project intentions to a distant place and for those intentions that need potent, fresh energy to achieve their goal.

Throughout the summer season a tree's energies are at their most puissant and influential. This is the season to source wood for workings that require mature, sophisticated dynamics. Complex castings and intricate workings are best served by living wands harvested in the summer.

The autumn season is a time when trees produce and distribute their reproductive seeds, fruits, acorns, and so forth. At this time, trees' spiritual energies are focused upon reproduction and future generations. Living wands harvested and used during autumn are ideal for love workings, fertility intentions, and the casting of regenerative magic. These wands are particularly appropriate for sex magic and fertility rites.

Winter-harvested wands, though crafted from dormant trees, are most often crafted for regenerative and potential growth workings, though for the most part they are not as potent as autumn-harvested wands. Wands harvested during the winter season from evergreens are ideal for longevity castings, endurance workings, and binding intentions (those intended to bind together individuals or objects).

The turning of the seasons also produces the most auspicious days, nights, sunrises, and sunsets of the year, on the the summer and winter solstices and the spring and autumn equinoxes. Workings and castings undertaken on these days and nights—particularly at sunrise and sunset—are by far the most potent and influential. The moon's phases are similarly intertwined with the passing of time and the seasons. As the moon waxes and wanes its influence varies in accordance with its appearance. Delicate, intricate workings are best undertaken under a thin moon, while workings under the fat moon are most wholesome and virtuous. To influence your workings with these seasonal connections it is important to consider them when you are seeking a branch to harvest and craft into a living wand.

Weather

The final external influence pertinent to choosing a donor branch that we need to consider is weather. Prevailing weather conditions are a major contributing factor in defining a tree's growing environment. As well as being affected by the changing seasons, prevailing weather may be subject to the donor tree's exact growing location, its proximity to the sea or large expanses of water, its height above sea level, the compass direction of its growth, and its general exposure to the elements.

Weather patterns can affect a tree's general growth and well-being, as we have discussed above. Moreover, weather conditions at the moment of a branch's harvesting also affect the wood's spiritual characteristics. Branches harvested on dry, calm days are not directly influenced by the weather. Consequently, we can expect them to exhibit the undisturbed attributes of the selected tree. Branches harvested in rainy conditions may have diluted attributes and they may not be as potent when used as living wands. Wands crafted from branches harvested during thunderstorms, however, are considered to be very powerful, with their attributes enhanced considerably. Furthermore, branches harvested during lightning storms have the most potent, vital energies, as their attributes are amplified by the energies of the lightning. *Lightning wands,* as they are called, are the most sought-after magical devices within the Druidic tradition.

HARVESTING RITE

We have seen above that harvesting the most appropriate branch from which to craft a living wand is far more complex than finding a tree of a chosen species and cutting off a random branch as you may be passing. The influencing factors detailed above must *all* be considered, and the harvesting must be scrupulously planned and executed.

It must be accepted that certain magical workings and castings cannot be undertaken during certain seasons of the year, as all living wands *must* be used as soon as possible following their harvesting. This means no more than six hours after they are cut from the donor tree. Also, even after the most meticulous planning, weather conditions may change at the last moment thereby influencing the harvesting for better or worse.

Harvesting, then, must be a well-planned, well-considered activity.

It takes time to choose the tree species that will enhance the intended influence the adept is planning, to balance its external influences in a way that will improve its overall effectiveness, and to decide upon the most appropriate season and time to harvest it. Choosing the individual branch to harvest requires an equal amount of reflection and consideration. Only when *all* of these variables have been considered and resolved in a balanced way can the adept turn her attention to the actual harvesting method itself.

The essential equipment for the harvesting rite, including a compass to establish the orientation of the donor tree and the selected branch.
(See also color plate 1.)

The *harvesting rite* is a profound ritual that, like all Druidic rites, is maintained primarily by an inherited oral tradition. The tradition requires performing detailed sequential actions in order to maintain the harvested branch's integrity and potency. Once all of the harvesting considerations above have been resolved, the adept may begin preparations for the harvesting.

The materials required include:

- A sharp ritual knife with which to cut away the branch. (An adept's typical cache of implements should contain such a ritual knife.)
- A thick, lightproof cloth in which to wrap the harvested branch. (Often made from wool, velvet, or similar.)
- A stick of sealing wax or a beeswax candle, used to seal the open wound left on the tree after the branch has been cut away and to seal the end of the harvested branch in order to retain its living sap and intrinsic spiritual energies.
- A container of pure sea salt, sufficient to cast a protective circle around the donor tree.

With these materials at hand the rite begins with the adept casting a protective circle around the donor tree, using the purifying salt and standing within the circle before invoking an intention of purification. For a detailed explanation of casting protective circles see page 59 in chapter four.

A brief note on Druidic intentions. We have seen earlier, that in the context of ancient Druidic lore, an *intention* is the equivalent of what may be called a *spell* in other traditions. It is cast in a similar way as a spell but is considered to project and bind the adept's intention to the chosen person, object, or location. Unlike spells, Druidic intentions are not learned by rote and recited. Each is individually composed in a way that reflects both the intended effect of the working and the personality of the adept herself. These two aspects are inseparable in any working and must work in a sympathetic and symbiotic way. The appropriate intention is most often composed as part of the preparations for the particular rite and will differ on each and every occasion.

A typical *intention of purification* may be similar to the following:

> As always, I thank nature for her abundant and
> precious gifts and ask once again that this sacred
> space be cleansed and purified, casting out all
> negative and harmful influences and creating a pure
> place within which my workings may thrive and
> produce benefit for all.

After invoking an intention of purification, remaining inside the protective circle of salt, it is now necessary for the adept to communicate directly with the chosen donor tree in order to explain what is about to happen and to seek assistance in ensuring that no harm comes to the tree, the harvested branch, or the adept herself. The primary point of engagement between two spiritual energies is found at the base of the spine, in direct line with the focal point of spiritual awareness—the brain. Having achieved a calm, meditative state, the adept sits in position with the base of her spine in direct contact with the tree's trunk. In this posture, she meditates upon the harvesting of the branch, sharing her inner thoughts and spiritual energies with those of the tree, while at the same time opening her own spiritual energies to receive those of the tree and achieve a state of spiritual communication.

Once satisfied that a state of understanding has been reached, the adept stands, picks up her ritual knife, and cuts away the targeted branch with a single firm cut. The length of the harvested branch should be approximately equal to the distance between the elbow and the tip of the extended middle finger of the adept's right arm. While holding the branch, seal both the cut end and the tree's wound with the sealing wax or beeswax. Then immediately wrap the cut branch in the protective cloth. With this, the harvesting is complete, the protective circle is erased, and the branch is taken to the adept's workshop where the cleansing and crafting of the living wand may proceed.

PURIFYING AND CLEANSING

Even having used stringent harvesting practices, it is still possible that the harvested branch may be affected by impurities accumulated during its growth. Even though care must be taken in selecting the specific branch from which the wand is to be crafted, it may not always be possible to identify every impurity it may have absorbed. So it is essential to cleanse each branch before crafting and using it. This cleansing working is common to all types of wands and must also apply to any other botanicals that may be incorporated into the final wand.

The particular method of cleansing that the adept employs is important. It seeks to spiritually cleanse the branch(es) and/or botanicals without reducing their spiritual energies in any way. The typical cleansing methods of water, fire, and smoke, used within the Druidic tradition, are not appropriate to cleanse wood for a living wand as they will interfere with or dilute the energies we seek to retain. Instead, we use salt, mint, or lavender as cleansing agents. The working includes immersing the branch(es) and/or botanicals in a layer of the chosen cleansing agent or a carefully crafted combination of some or all of the agents. The individual agents are selected for their unique virtues, defined as follows:

Salt: The strongest yet harshest of the cleansing agents. Used primarily where a powerful cleansing is needed, or when the adept is unsure of what may have contaminated the branch. Salt is not a subtle agent but does remove any and all contaminants that may be present.

Mint: A powerful but less aggressive cleansing agent than salt. Used when specific contaminants are known and require a potent agent to remove them.

Lavender: The most subtle of cleansing agents. Typically used in situations where the provenance of the branch (its origin and how it has been handled since it was harvested) is well known and the branch is free of any damaging influences. It is good practice to cleanse every harvested branch or botanical with lavender as a safeguard against any random potential contaminant that may have influenced it during its lifetime, harvesting, or temporary storage.

If salt is being used, it must be pure sea salt, either directly evaporated from fresh seawater by the adept (this is the preferred method) or acquired from a source with known provenance. If either mint or lavender are being used, they must be newly harvested by the adept and be of known provenance and purity (i.e., you know the location, time, and method of harvesting). Store-bought dried or fresh herbs are not acceptable as they are ineffective.

The Cleansing Working

The *cleansing working* is a simple one. It begins by placing a layer of the cleansing agent, slightly wider and longer than the item being cleansed, on your working stone. If the adept does not have access to a traditional working stone, then another work surface is fine. The item to be cleansed is then placed on top of the bed of salt or herbs and covered with the remaining cleansing agent so that it is completely immersed. Leave the covered branch and/or botanical beneath the cleansing agent for a minimum of two hours. The branch or botanical must then be used for wand crafting *immediately* after it is removed from the salt or herb in order to avoid any ambient contamination. Afterward, return the cleansing agent to the earth. It may not be reused for any sort of working as it has absorbed the spiritual contamination it has cleansed from the original branch or botanical. Once the adept has completed this cleansing working, the harvested branch or other botanicals are now ready for crafting.

CRAFTING OVERVIEW

Workspace, Tools, and Woodcraft Techniques

There is nothing unusual about the materials needed to craft a living wand. Everything required should be within the typical cache of the adept. The *crafting working* must be undertaken within a cleansed and protected workshop or workspace. The adept may use the same ritual knife for the crafting that was used for the harvesting, and the original protective cloth that held the harvested branch may be used to protect the final living wand.

Unlike intricately turned deadwood wands, there are no complicated or sophisticated turning or carving skills needed to craft a living wand. As the surface of the living wand remains in its original state throughout, there is also no need for specialist surface finishing, varnishing, or waxing following the crafting.

Initial Meditation and Visualization

As with all workings of Druidic crafting, nothing is begun until a clear and detailed vision of the finished objective is firmly set in the adept's mind. This is achieved through a process of meditation and visualization. Only once this is achieved may the crafting of the living wand begin.

The first step in this process is to establish a calm, meditative state of mind and spirit. There are a vast variety of techniques to establish a relaxed and calm state of being, such as breath awareness and progressive muscle relaxation. Once a meditative state has been achieved, progress to the next stage.

The objective of the meditative visualization is to mentally proceed through each stage of the crafting, anticipating any likely difficulties, resolving them, and stepping through every stage of the process from beginning to end in one's mind. The stages for crafting a living wand are few, and the potential difficulties are easy to overcome. The first is the removal of the branch from the protective cloth, and the last is rewrapping the completed living wand with this same cloth. Only once the adept has each and every step of the crafting firmly implanted in her consciousness can the actual physical crafting begin.

Translation and Crafting

Now the adept must translate her meditative visualization into the physical crafting of the living wand. Within the same protective workshop or workspace, remove the harvested branch from its protective wrapping and place it on the working stone. Again, your work surface may be an actual working stone or a simple workbench or table.

First remove any extraneous growths or deposits (fungi, bird droppings, any foreign-body attachments) from the branch using the ritual knife. Then, using the same knife, cut the sealing wax or beeswax away from the harvested end of the branch in a diagonal cut, exposing the sap and inner layers of the branch. The aim is to create a slanting surface of exposed sap and sapwood that will come into direct contact with the adept's hand as the intention is cast, thereby creating a direct route for the spiritual energies of the adept to travel from her core toward the intended recipient or object. Note that after making this diagonal cut, the vulnerable living sap and core of the wand are exposed to the elements; this allows the living elements of the wand to evaporate and degenerate. It is imperative that cutting the wax from the harvested end of the branch is done at the last possible moment before the wand is to be used. At this moment the living wand is at its most powerful.

Storage and Maintenance

Although we have established that every living wand must be used as soon as possible following its harvesting and crafting, there may on occasion be a brief interlude between crafting and the actual casting of the intention for which the wand was created. In such cases the wand must be securely bound in its protective wrapping until it is to be used. If circumstances prescribe that there may be a protracted period between the crafting and the casting, the wand may be cleansed of any unwanted external influences by unwrapping its protective cover, pouring in enough pure sea salt to envelope the wand, and rewrapping the protective cover to secure the wand and the salt. The wand should remain in the salt wrap for a minimum of ten minutes in order for the sea salt to effectively cleanse the wand's spiritual energies. Afterward the wand may be used as explained in chapter seven, "Using Your Wand." This sea salt cleansing should only be used in unanticipated circumstances and never if a period of more than six hours has passed since the harvesting and crafting of the wand. It will not revitalize a wand that has been harvested more than six hours ago. One of the functions of sea salt cleansing is to stimulate the sap within the wand, but this sap is no longer a living energy after the six-hour period has elapsed.

THREE

WOOD TYPES

Attributes and Virtues of Ten Species

Almost every spiritual tradition around the globe acknowledges the importance of the spiritual energies of trees. Most traditions embrace this belief by harnessing and utilizing these energies in one form or another. The most typical means of accessing these energies is through the use of wands, staffs, rods, and similar wooden devices, each establishing an empathetic connection between the ritual device and its user. Most traditions agree that different tree species have inherent attributes and virtues that vary from species to species. We can see these ancient beliefs within various cultures' folk traditions, healing traditions, and spiritual traditions, both formal and informal. Some of these traditions have informed modern medicine and advances in chemistry and scientific understanding throughout the world, while other ancient discoveries are still used in fabric dyes, culinary flavorings, and holistic healing therapies.

Along with unique physical characteristics, each tree species has its own spiritual energies. Some are positive, while others may be less so. We will be exploring these unique spiritual attributes and virtues in this chapter.

With an awareness that each tree has its own characteristic attributes, Druidic adepts have long selected specific tree species for specific applications, knowing that the chosen tree will add its spiritual energies to those of the adept as she strives to address the needs of her community. While in the previous chapter we have examined the external influences affecting the individual tree from which we intend to harvest a living wand, here we concern ourselves only with the spiritual attributes and internal virtues of the tree types. These spiritual and internal attributes depend upon the tree itself, which is the primary reason we focus firstly and so intently upon the donor tree; the donor tree will always be the overwhelming influence on the final living wand when it is used. To reiterate, it is imperative that the adept has a thorough understanding of the external influences on the attributes and virtues of each tree species. There is little or no point in crafting a wand from any other wood than that which has been harvested from a living tree by the adept herself, and using any wood imported from outside the adept's indigenous environment will be ineffective. To maximize the potency of a Druidic living wand, the adept must have intimate familiarity with the attributes of the tree species that provides the donor branch and she must use wood from the natural environment to which she is connected.

We will focus our exploration of the spiritual attributes and virtues of particular species of trees on a range of the most familiar trees that grow in the ancient Druidic regions of Northern Europe and the British Isles. It is beyond the purview of this book to instruct the reader on how to identify individual species of trees in the wild. There are many varied resources, including field guides and more, designed specifically to aid in identifying the trees in every region of the world. I refer each reader to their own excellent local resource.

In the following sections we will establish a detailed directory of the most common trees used within the Druidic tradition. We will identify their individual spiritual attributes and virtues, their history and background within the tradition, and recommendations for their most appropriate applications when crafting Druidic living wands as defined by the oral tradition of the Druids of Wales and Ireland. Names of the trees in the native languages of the Druidic homelands are also provided. Readers may wish to use these authentic names in their workings.

As we explore each of the ten selected species, we will look at their individual internal attributes and virtues while ignoring the external influences explained in the previous chapter. It is, however, imperative to also consider these external influences before any individual donor tree is identified.

APPLE

The single variety of apple tree native to Britain is the crab apple—a small tree with brown, flaky bark, sometimes bearing the thorns all crab apples once had, being of the rose family. The small bitter fruit can be made into jam, jelly, and wine and is food for many birds and animals, including mice, voles, foxes, badgers, rabbits, deer, and, of course, wild boar. Revered by the Druids as one of the seven chief trees and the most common one to host mistletoe, the apple tree is associated with shapeshifting and journeys to the otherworld. Magical apple trees feature in many folk and fairy tales throughout the world. The name Avalon, the mythical island featured in Arthurian legend, is derived from an Old Irish word meaning "place of apple trees"; in this context, the apple tree symbolizes the hardship, sacrifice, and self-denial that the ancient warrior/magician has to undergo to make the journey to Avalon. Apple was considered a food of the gods and a universal symbol of love, fertility, generosity, and abundance.

The apple tree and its fruit play a significant role in Druidic lore. They are acknowledged as symbols of fruitfulness, wisdom, and plenty. The wood of the apple tree has many practical applications, and its fruits are used in the fermentation of a number of spiritual and ritual drinks and potions. Applewood living wands are one of the most frequently used within the Druidic tradition, as their attributes are sympathetic with many of the intentions and workings of the pagan community.

The proto-Celtic name for apple is *aballā*. In Old Irish it is either *uball* or *ubull*, while in modern Irish it is rendered as *ubhal* or *úll*. In Scottish Gaelic it is *ubhall;* in Manx, *ooyl;* in Welsh, *afal;* and in Cornish and Bretton, *aval*.

Apple wood is used in ritual fires of purification at the entry portals to stone circles. And it is used in rites of passage rituals for young women, imbuing them with fertility, fruitfulness, and wisdom. Garlands of apple branches are used to secure protective ritual spaces.

As with oak (page 46), the apple tree's attributes are sympathetic with a wide range of applications. Living wands crafted from its wood are used for a great variety of purposes. Most importantly, applewood living wands are used in castings of intentions that are amplified by the attributes of fertility, fruitfulness, and wisdom. And they are particularly associated with applications by female adepts or ones directed to female recipients.

BIRCH, SILVER

The silver birch is another sacred tree in Druidic lore, symbolizing knowledge, inspiration, and protection. Birch trees are hardy and adaptable; they grow where many other trees cannot. Silver birch seldom grows alone and is often found in groves. These, like the better-known oak groves, are a focal point for Druidic ritual.

In proto-Celtic birch is known as *betuyā*. In Scottish Gaelic the silver birch is known as *beith;* in Manx, *beih;* in Welsh, *bedw;* in Cornish, *besewen;* in Breton, *bezv;* in Old Irish, *beithe;* and in modern Irish, *beith*.

Birchwood living wands are associated with purification and protection. Birchwood brooms are used to drive away the unwanted energies of the old year in a protective ritual called *beating the bounds,* which is still conducted in many rural villages and homelands throughout Wales, Scotland, and Cornwall. Newborn cradles are still often made of birch wood for these same protective qualities, and it is said that carrying a piece of birch will protect you from the "little folk," the mischievous fairy folk of the Druidic homelands that include the leprechaun, cluricaun, and Fir Dureg of Irish tradition. In ancient times stripped, pressed, and dried silver birch bark was used as parchment. Known in Welsh as *Memrwn y Derwyddon,* or "Druid's parchment," sheets crafted in this manner were used for drawn or written curses and intentions, and some still exist in the National Museums of Wales archives.

The birch tree is also used to make maypoles to celebrate the coming of spring. And flaming torches of birch are used to start the fires to celebrate Beltane, the Gaelic festival of new beginnings and abundant crops that occurs in May.

In spring, birch sap may be drawn out of the trunk and made into a delicious, spiritually potent mead and fortified with carefully chosen botanicals to be used in many ritual draughts, the drinks taken during rituals and celebrations.

Silver birch living wands are used to cast highly protective influences. In Herefordshire, England, trees are still decorated with red and white rags then propped against stable doors to ward off evil on May Day each year.

ELM, WYCH

There are three species of elm growing in the Druidic heartlands: wych, English, and field. Wych elm is the only truly native elm.

The wood of the elm is flexible, which is reflected in the Old English word *wice,* meaning "supple." This became *wiche* in Middle English and eventually *wych* in its modern usage. In proto-Celtic the word for elm is *lēmos;* in Old Irish it is *lem;* in modern Irish, *leamhán leathan;* in Scottish Gaelic, *eamhan mòr;* in Manx, *lhiouan;* in Welsh, *llwyfen wych;* in Cornish, *elow;* and in Breton, *evlec'h.*

Wych elm trees are often found growing in graveyards in Ireland alongside the ubiquitous yew. Traditionally, most coffins are made from elm wood, mainly because of its resistance to water. In Wales, medieval archers chose elm to craft their longbows, while across the border in England yew was the wood of choice. Across Britain remains of elmwood bows have been found in burial sites from the Mesolithic Age (or Middle Stone Age) alongside other ancient elmwood tools and artifacts.

Elmwood living wands have the attributes of wisdom, good health, dedication, and commitment.

HAWTHORN

The hawthorn tree, or May tree, is known today throughout the Druidic homelands as the fairy tree. In the month of May it blooms with prolific white flowers. In local folklore it is also often called the gentle bush, the lone bush, and the solitary thorn, mainly because it is thought to be disrespectful to mention its fairy name out loud.

Cutting a hawthorn tree down or harvesting its branches is believed to attract extremely bad luck. In fact, it is considered unlucky to disturb the hawthorn in any way for fear of upsetting the "little folk" who inhabit the tree. These fairy beliefs are so deeply rooted that in 1999 work was interrupted on the main road from Limerick to Galway in Ireland because a fairy tree (hawthorn) stood in its path. The road was subsequently rerouted, and construction was delayed for ten years. Single hawthorn trees, standing alone, are considered to be the most precious to the fairy folk and as such they must never be disturbed for fear of attracting the fairies' wrath.

In Druidic lore, the hawthorn tree is often known as the Queen of the May. It is respected for its unique beauty and its ability to support so many forms of wildlife and birds. Its abundant blossoms represent the end of the long, dark winter and the beginning of spring, with its burgeoning new life and fertility.

In Scottish Gaelic the hawthorn is known as *Haw droigheann*. In Manx it is known as *daragh;* in Welsh, *Ddraenen wen;* in Cornish, *derowen;* in Breton, *elorriarra;* and in Old and modern Irish, *Hauth* or *sceach gheal.*

Many of the ancient Druidic stone circles have hawthorn trees growing next to their periphery. The hawthorn trees are often adorned with strips of rag or ribbons, called *wish rags* or *wish ribbons*. These are tied to the tree as a wish is recited; as the rag or ribbon decays and falls to the ground, the wish will slowly take effect.

The hawthorn tree is believed to be the giver and taker of life. Hawthorn's beautiful flowers are believed to smell of death, as the plant shares some of the chemical components found in rotting flesh. In medieval times, the arrival of the plague was associated with foul smells, such as open sewers, quite rightly so as we later discovered. The noxious smell of the hawthorn blossom too came to be associated with the arrival of the bubonic plague. As a giver of life, hawthorn trees are also well known, providing homes for a wide variety of local wildlife that nest and make their habitats in their foliage and among their roots. Hawthorn trees produce berries, called haws, that ripen slowly, turning from springtime green to a deep red in autumn. The berries persist throughout autumn and often into winter, providing food for country folk, like wild animals and birds.

The hawthorn tree, with its sharp, thorny branches, embodies the attributes of protection and safety. Hawthorn branches are traditionally hung above doors, windows, and entrances to prevent malevolent influences from entering. Crowns of hawthorn are still worn by brides as a sign of fertility, while burning torches of hawthorn traditionally illuminated wedding rites. This tradition may be the origin of the phrase *carrying a torch* for a potential lover, meaning to have strong emotional attraction to another.

Living wands crafted from hawthorn wood amplify intentions cast to secure fertility, affection, kind thoughts, and protection. Conversely, living wands crafted from thorny hawthorn branches are used to cast curses, malevolent desires, and even death curses.

HAZEL

The hazel tree is significant in Druidic lore for both its wood and its nuts. Remains of both have been discovered in ritual sites and burial tombs throughout Wales, Ireland, Scotland, and England.

The proto-Celtic name for hazel is *koslos,* while in both Old Irish and modern Irish it is *coll.* In Scottish Gaelic, it is either *call* or *calltuinn;* in Manx, it is *coull;* and in Welsh, *collen.* In the ancient language of Cornish it is *collwedhen,* and in the Breton language of Northern France it is *kraoñklevezenn.*

Hazel is often associated with witchcraft. In both Wales and Ireland it is considered to be a fairy tree, reputedly a home to fairy folk, and its wood is still used to craft dowsing rods, which are used to find sources of underground water.

In the Druidic tradition, hazel is considered to be the tree of inspiration. Hazelwood living wands are used to inspire creative thought. For the same reason, the hazel tree is acknowledged as the tree of bards, poets, and writers. As such, hazel wood is never used as firewood, either in the hearth or in ritual fires. Hazelwood wands are still favored by witches and practitioners of other nature-based pagan belief systems.

In the Cornish Druidic tradition we still find hazelwood branches being used in conjunction with *millpreve,* traditional objects akin to the adder stones of the Welsh. An adder stone is a small, smooth circular stone with a naturally occurring hole in it. Seen as a rare gift from nature, adder stones are used in Druidic rituals and sometimes worn around the neck on a leather cord in order to strengthen an individual's connection to sacred nature. In the Cornish Druidic tradition, a hazel living wand may have a millpreve threaded on to it near its base, forming a guard-like barrier between the adept's hand and the shaft of the wand, using the millpreve's natural energies to enhance the wand's potency.

In rural Welsh folklore, when a person wished to finish a romantic relationship, he or she would give their rejected partner a twig of hazel with its leaves still attached and the relationship would come to an end as the leaves fell from the twig.

Historically, great store was also placed on the hazelnut. As well as providing a valuable source of foraged food, the nuts were believed to be the receptacle of great knowledge; they were often known as the *nuts of wisdom*. References to the wisdom acquired from the hazelnut may be found in many folktales and mythical stories of Wales and Ireland.

The hazel tree's virtues of wisdom, knowledge, and reasoning make it an ideal wood from which to craft living wands that benefit from such attributes.

HOLLY

Like some other trees native to the Druidic heartlands, holly trees have protective properties and are frequently left uncut in natural hedges. A more arcane reason for this was to obstruct witches who were known to run along the tops of hedges during their nightly journeys. More practically, farmers use their easily identifiable evergreen shapes to establish their furrows in straight lines during their winter plowing.

The holly tree is one of the most respected trees in Druidic lore, and it is the evergreen twin of the oak tree. While the oak tree is seen as the most influential of all trees during the light half of the year, the holly tree influences the dark, winter months. Holly trees symbolize peace, security, and goodwill. When planted near dwellings they protect against damage from lightning strikes. In the Druidic tradition, living wands crafted from holly wood invoke protective qualities, guarding against malevolent energies and ill fortune.

Early chieftains, the elected leaders of the ancient tribes of the Druidic homelands, wore holly wreath crowns as an emblem of good fortune, protection, and power. In the same way, newborn babies were washed in "holly water" baths, made by macerating holly leaves in spring water, in order to imbue them with health and good fortune and protect them from harm.

The proto-Celtic name for holly is *kolinnos*. In Scottish Gaelic, it is *Chuillin;* in Manx, *daragh;* in Welsh, *Celun;* in Cornish, *kelynnen;* in Breton, *kelenenn;* in Old Irish, *cuilenn;* and in modern Irish, *Cuileann.*

Holly leaves and garlands and its bright red berries add color to the dark days of Yule. This pre-Christian, pagan practice continues to the present day with "the holly and the ivy" still being a principal image of Christmas—historically a boy decked with holly leaves and a girl with ivy, paraded around the village as a sign of summer fruitfulness and evergreen nature during the darkest part of the year. In the Welsh tradition, each year holly was brought into the home, defining who would rule the household for the following year. If prickly-leaved branches were brought in first, the man would rule the home; if the first branches held smooth leaves, then the woman would rule the home. Druidic tradition holds that holly wood possesses potent protective qualities and guards against evil energies and the dark work of witchcraft and sorcery.

OAK

There is no tree more closely associated with the Druidic tradition than the oak. The proto-Celtic word for oak is *daru, derwā,* or most often *duir.* It is suggested that the word *Druid* is derived from one or another of these words and thereby translates as "knower of the oak tree." In the tradition of the Druids of Wales and Ireland, the oak tree is associated with energy, strength, and longevity, as well as truth, wisdom, and courage. The ancient Druids were known to practice their rites in groves of oaks and typically crafted powerful wands and staffs from oakwood branches.

In Scottish Gaelic, the name for oak is *daraich;* in Manx, it is *daragh;* in Welsh, *derwen;* in Cornish, *derowen;* in Breton, *dervenn;* and in Old and modern Irish, it is *dair.*

The most magical plant of the Druidic tradition, mistletoe, is at its most potent when it grows on an oak tree, and it is harvested as one of the most precious botanicals in Druidic lore. Oak leaves and mistletoe are used to craft ritual headdresses. It is believed that mistletoe, a parasitic plant, is placed on the oak's branches by nature during lightning strikes and that its vibrant white berries contain the bright white light of the energy of the lightning itself.

The oak tree is arguably the hardiest of the Druidic heartlands' native tree species and has many practical applications. Ancient oaks still remain, particularly in the mixed woodlands of Wales and Ireland where some of Europe's largest oak forests may be found. Unfortunately, many of the indigenous English oak forests were felled over many years to produce wood for England's famous military naval fleet.

Oak trees are known to live extremely long lives and to grow into huge mature trees. These major oaks are sacred to the pagan Druidic community. In Wales and Ireland major oaks may be found with Druidic symbols carved into their bark. Some of these carvings are hundreds of years old and frequently relate to images of long life and immortality.

Oakwood living wands add strength and durability to any working for which they are used. They are considered to be the most versatile of all Druidic living wands. They embody the attributes of longevity, strength, veracity, dedication, profundity, truth, and commitment.

PINE, SCOTS

Pine trees are among the oldest seed-bearing plants on our planet and appear to have existed for over 300 million years. Pine trees were one of the first tree species to populate the British Isles and Ireland, and the Scots pine is the only pine tree native to the island of Ireland. Large, mature Scots pine trees are seen everywhere in the landscape of Scotland, where they were planted as wayside markers for travelers and as markers of the burial places of heroic warriors and chieftains. The Scots pine remains the emblem of a number of Scottish clans. Across the rest of the British Isles, they were used as markers along drove roads, special routes for cattle, to mark the way to markets and grazing meadows.

The proto-Celtic name for the pine is *k^w resnom.* In Old Irish and modern Irish, it is *peine albanach;* in Scottish Gaelic, *giuthas;* in Manx, *croan;* in Welsh, *pinwydd yr Alban;* and in Breton, *pinua.*

In Druidic tradition all evergreen pines represent continuity of life through the long, dark, and cold winter months. Juxtaposing the yew tree, which represents death and decay, the pine tree represents new birth, continuity, and the persistence of the warm, sunny summer. As a result, pine ritual fires are lit throughout the winter to entice the sun to return, and the fires' ashes are scattered on the soil to ensure fertility and good crops.

Because of the association of pine trees with the bright summer months and with continuity through the winter, torches of pine wood are used for rituals during winter and frequently illuminate stone circles, along with pine wood that is used in purification fires at the circles' entry portals. As trees of light, in pagan tradition pine trees are decorated with shiny, bright objects to acknowledge their attributes. Although the tradition of the decorated pine Christmas tree at the height of the winter solstice is only a few hundred years old, the relationship with the ancient pagan tradition of decorating pine trees is not difficult to understand. The older, northern tradition of the Yule log is also a remnant from the same pagan ritual and it is traditionally crafted from pine wood.

Pinecones may be carried to increase fertility and vigor, and the smoke from the massive pinewood bonfires of the Druids is considered to be both cleansing and energizing. Every stone circle is cleansed by a pinewood fire on each solstice and equinox.

Living wands crafted from Scots pine have the attributes of longevity, brightness, fertility, renewal, and persistence, each reflecting the evergreen character of the tree.

ROWAN

The rowan tree, also known as the mountain ash or quicken tree, is another important tree in Druidic lore and a favorite for crafting living wands. While its branches are frequently harvested for wand crafting, rowan wood is never, ever cut for firewood, even when wood is scarce, for fear of having one's home and family consumed by fire.

The proto-Celtic name for rowan is *osnistū*. In Old Irish, it is *fuinnseóc;* in modern Irish, *fuinseog;* in Scottish Gaelic, *fuinnseann;* in Manx, *unjin;* in Welsh, *onnen;* in Cornish, *onnen;* and in Breton, *onn.*

Along with hazel and hawthorn trees, rowan trees are considered by followers of witchcraft and fairy folk to be part of the magical trilogy of fairy lore. Rowanwood living wands have the power to ward off fairies and malignant energies. A potion containing rowan sap is used as a protection against witchcraft and conjurers. The wood of the rowan tree is seen as the most potent element. It is used for stirring milk to prevent it curdling; for crafting brewing wands for making ale, mead, and *metheglyn* (an ancient form of medicinal or magic mead popular within the Welsh Druidic tradition); and for crafting divining rods, also known as dowsing rods.

YEW

The yew tree has a well-established reputation as a long-lived tree. It is believed that it can survive for over 9,500 years, although it is difficult to confirm this phenomenal age due to the unique way in which the tree reproduces and grows, with new growth emerging from the remains of the dead trunk.

The yew tree is well established in the Druidic lore of all of the British Isles, where it is known by a variety of names. Its proto-Celtic name is *eburos;* in Scottish Gaelic, it is *iubhar;* in Manx, *euar;* in Welsh, *ywen;* in Cornish, *ewen;* in Breton, *heuor;* in Old Irish, *Ibar;* and in modern Irish, *Iúr.* Throughout the many rural regions of the British Isles, the yew tree is also known by a great number of regional and local folk names.

It is perhaps the longevity of yew trees and their rather strange way of regenerating that made the yew tree sacred to the way of life of pagan Druids, becoming appropriated later by the early Christian fathers who introduced Christianity to the British Isles. Yew trees were seen as being immortal. Pagan Druids likely appreciated their unique ability to grow their branches down into the earth to form new trees, many of which twist together surrounding the original trunk. As old branches die new life can form within them. A yew tree that looks old and withered is constantly renewing itself. As a result, the trunks can grow to be massive in diameter.

Almost every part of the yew tree is poisonous, suggesting how it may have gained its reputation as the death tree. Very little can grow underneath the canopy of a yew tree as it sheds a dense carpet of poisonous needles, killing any competitive growth, while its impenetrable canopy prevents any sunlight from reaching the forest floor. During the turbulent times of the Roman and Viking invasions, indigenous British tribes were known to poison themselves with a potion derived from yew trees rather than surrender to or be subjugated by their enemy.

The county and town of Mayo (*Maigh Eo*) in Ireland translates as "Plains of the Yew Trees" and was known to be the home of the largest yew forest in the world. Commonly, yew trees seldom form forests but prefer to grow individually or in small groves. In Ireland, Scotland, and Wales we find numerous examples of ancient Christian churches with single yews growing in their confines, while other churches are surrounded by a small group of yew trees which would once have been a sacred tree grove, a place of worship for the ancient Druids and their communities. Many yew trees are found growing at crossroads, having been used as wayside markers for travelers and meeting places for the local community. The same locations were used by early Christian church builders, which may account for why we see so many yew trees in today's churchyards. Some suggest that yew trees may also have been planted in church burial grounds to deter wild animals from digging up newly-buried corpses, as a result of their shedding of their poisonous needles.

One of the oldest surviving man-made objects found in the Druidic heartlands is a spearhead crafted from yew wood, dating back at least 150,000 years. In later days, yew was the wood most frequently used to make longbows due to its strength and durability. The wood of the yew is among the hardest known woods; it is so dense that it sinks in water. The same archers tipped their arrows with the toxic sap of the yew in order to poison their enemies.

The spiritual characteristics of the yew tree are well known in the Druidic tradition. Yew trees symbolize death, resurrection, permanence, longevity, security, and trust. Living wands crafted from yew wood will convey these attributes. Because of the way the needles of the yew grow along its branches, it can be difficult to find a branch that is suitable to craft into a living wand. Careful attention, however, will reveal an appropriate candidate. *Warning:* Again, almost every part of the yew tree is poisonous; great care should be taken when handling *any and all* parts of the tree.

SUMMARY

The ten trees we have looked at are arguably the most significant in the Druidic tradition. As we have seen, each has its own individual attributes and virtues that will enhance any appropriate and sympathetic working. Choosing the right wood with which to craft a living wand for any specific casting is dependent upon the attributes the adept is seeking. The group of trees detailed above represents a wide range of attributes that may enhance and amplify the most frequently encountered needs in everyday life. Having said that, we will encounter other tree species, bushes, and botanicals as we progress through the following chapters of this book. These have been included in order to illustrate the versatility of living wands in a broader context.

Most importantly, as a recap of our exploration so far, it is essential to identify the virtues and attributes of each species as the first step in finding the most appropriate tree for crafting and using a living wand. Only when the adept is familiar with the virtues and attributes of different species can she begin the task of searching for the perfect donor tree within the forested landscape. We can see, then, that becoming intimately familiar with the forest panorama is the initial aim: knowing which trees grow where, what external influences and seasonal variations may be affecting a tree's spiritual attributes, and so forth. As we have discussed, every tree has its own individual physical characteristics, its material presence; its share of the universal communal energy that identifies it as a tree (as opposed to a flower or other type of botanical); and its own individual or personal energy that defines it as a specific, individual tree and separates it from all the other individual trees in the forest. These three components are its cardinal essences within the Druidic tradition, the three basic building blocks of all Druidic botanical lore. We will see later in this book how these cardinal essences may be channeled, amplified, and employed in order to enhance each living wand in its intended use.

WOOD QUALITIES REFERENCE CHART

Wood Type	Attributes and Virtues
Apple	Fertility, fruitfulness, wisdom; associated with the feminine as well as shapeshifting and magical journeys
Birch, Silver	Knowledge, inspiration, purification, protection
Elm, Wych	Wisdom, good health, dedication, commitment
Hawthorn	Fertility, affection, kind thoughts, protection; the giver and taker of life
Hazel	Inspiration, creativity, reasoning
Holly	Protection, peace, security, goodwill
Oak	Energy, strength, longevity, truth, wisdom, courage
Pine, Scots	Fertility, new birth, continuity, persistence
Rowan	Protection, guardianship, divination, insight
Yew	Death, resurrection, permanence, longevity, security, trust

Choosing the ideal donor tree, identifying the ideal branch, harvesting the branch, and crafting the living wand is not a simple series of tasks. Doing all of these steps while the branch is still alive, with all the vitality of the chosen tree species actively within it, is even more difficult. To achieve the desired result, the entire series of events must be meticulously planned and executed. In time, each forest grove, each tree species, and the prevailing external influences will become a natural extension of the adept's own spiritual personality. Begin this evolution with gentle walks in the forest, relaxing and meditating in the forest atmosphere. Absorb the spiritual energies of the forest; feel the difference in the spiritual energies of each species and then begin to focus on the physical aspects of the forested landscape, the location of different species and exactly where each individual species thrives. In time, your memory will absorb the location of each potential donor tree and more detailed insight into the trees' surrounding external influences will unfold. Eventually, an intimate understanding of each tree and its place in its forest home will develop, and each tree will become a trusted friend. It is then that a connection with the ancient ways will enter the adept's own spiritual being; a connection with the ancient pagan beliefs and the lore of the Druids will mature within the adept and with this connection and understanding she will grow and fulfill her role in nature's partnership.

Only when the adept thoroughly understands each of the principles described in the previous chapters should she begin her journey of crafting and using Druidic living wands. Taking these principles into account, it is difficult to understand the premise of store-bought wands or wands manufactured in bulk from stock supplies of wood or abandoned chairs. It is difficult to support the use of elaborately turned and decorated wands purchased from anonymous makers on the internet. What are the origins of any energies these sorts of wands contain, if any energies are present at all? If the adept respects the spiritual energies we have discussed, it is not possible to realistically expect these anonymous wands to influence her workings.

Once again, for a wand to exhibit any of the attributes and virtues of its donor tree it must still contain the living, vital sap, containing its physical and spiritual characteristics, of the living tree the branch was harvested from while acknowledging the external influences of the donor tree's growing environment. This cannot be the case with anonymous wands from unknown sources manufactured from dead wood that has long since lost its spiritual essences. By the same token, it is not possible to use a wand borrowed from another person for all the reasons we have just explored. Provenance is key and cannot be disregarded. Unless they are harvested and crafted by the user, while taking into account *all* of the principles detailed above, wands have little or no credibility within the lore of the Druid.

FOUR

WAND TYPES

Crafting Rudimentary, Entwined, and
Compound Wands, Rods, Staffs, and More

Often when people think of magic wands they think of either the comical black and white wand of the stage magician or the elaborately turned wands they see featured in many fantasy films. Few people are aware of the varied collection of practical, Druidic living wands that make up the principal magical devices still used today by the Druids of the British Isles and Ireland.

It is important to emphasize that Druidic living wands are only ever crafted from living wood, occasionally augmented with other living botanicals. They are *never* manufactured from other materials such as metal, crystal, or inorganic artificial substitutes. Neither are they ever embellished with crystals or anything other than living botanicals.

Unlike the black and white wands used by the stage conjurer or the decorative, crystal-tipped wands of the fictional apprentice wizards we all know and love, Druidic living wands are practical magical devices carefully crafted from specific woods to be used in very particular circumstances. Each has individual attributes and virtues, and each may be crafted in a distinct form in order to match the purpose for which it is fashioned. Each living wand is used only once.

Having explored in great detail the variety of woods that are utilized within the Druidic tradition and why each wood is selected for its anticipated use, we will now look at the various physical forms in which living wands may be crafted and why each form is uniquely appropriate for its intended application. Some forms are simple, others are much more complex, and some are defined by the physical structure of the tree or botanical from which the wood or botanical elements are harvested. The wand's physical form is as important as any other consideration in its crafting, and each form is rendered carefully and deliberately in order to embrace and enhance the adept's intended working or casting. The choice of which physical form is most appropriate is determined by thoughtful, informed consideration. In most cases, the final form will be one of the following wand types.

RUDIMENTARY WANDS

At its most basic, a wand is a thin, lightweight branch that is manipulated with one hand. Similarly, a simple stick was often used in primitive cultures for reaching, pointing, drawing in the dirt, and directing people; as such, it is one of the earliest and simplest tools known to people of all civilizations. Related magical devices include longer versions of the wand such as staffs, rods, and virges, along with more stylized, ceremonial staffs, such as scepters and crooks that are frequently used as symbols of rank and status.

In Druidic tradition, the *rudimentary wand,* as the name suggests, is a wand in its simplest form. It must be emphasized, however, that in this case, *simple* does not mean weak or insipid—quite the contrary. Rudimentary wands are typically some of the most potent and focused devices at the adept's disposal. Rudimentary wands are crafted from a freshly harvested branch from a single, carefully chosen

Rudimentary living wand. (See also color plate 2.)

tree, selected with the goal of enhancing the adept's intention or other
working by amplifying the energy of the working and imbuing it with
the attributes and virtues manifested in the wild tree.

Appropriate Uses for Rudimentary Wands

As a rudimentary wand is crafted from the wood of a single tree species, it carries the focused attributes of the chosen species, unaffected by any of the complex influences of additional tree species or botanicals. This gives the wand a unique focus and potency not found in more complicated types of wands or other magical devices.

Rudimentary wands are the most well known of all Druidic wands. In fact, many people are unaware that there are any other types. A single branch fashioned into a single-shaft wand allows the adept to concentrate the attributes of the tree species and direct them toward the intention's recipient, whether that is a person, object, or a location or space. Such wands are typically employed to cast simple yet powerful intentions, ones that would be diminished by the external influences of additional trees or botanicals.

Crafting a Rudimentary Wand for Casting

We will see as we progress through this chapter that although there are a number of various, more complex wand types, each wand type begins with one or more simple rudimentary wands, exactly like the one we shall be crafting in this section.

We begin this crafting with the chosen harvested branch held within its protective wrapping. The cut end of the wand is still sealed with the sealing wax used during the harvesting, and the *tip*, at the opposite end of the wand, remains in its original state. All extraneous growth and contamination (anything that is not a product of the branch's natural growth) will have been removed during the harvesting and the branch has been cleansed and purified (see page 32).

In order to maintain the spiritual integrity of a wand, it is imperative that the crafting, the last working to take place before the wand is used, be carried out inside a cleansed protective circle.

Protective Circles

We introduced the process of *casting a protective circle* in chapter two. Here we will discuss establishing these safe spaces in more detail, including the steps for casting a protective circle, sealing it, and then cleansing it.

Background
• • • • • • • •

Typically, all Druidic workings are carried out within the confines of a sealed and cleansed protective circle. Formal rituals are usually conducted within a large protective circle that, where possible, would be cast on the perimeter of a stone circle; in cases where casting such a circle is not possible, a similar circle is cast on flat ground. Ideal locations for these circles include forest groves, parkland, or even backyard gardens. For smaller, less formal workings, protective circles that are large enough to encircle the working space required are cast. In formal stone circles, rituals and workings are centered upon the *working stone*, most frequently a large recumbent stone situated opposite the entry portals and near the internal periphery of the circle. Unfortunately, most adepts will not have access to such ancient sites; even so, all protective circles are cast in a way that reproduces the essential elements of the original stone circle sites.

In many cases the working stone is replaced by a table or workbench in the confines of the adept's workshop, kitchen, or garden. (This will be discussed in more detail in the following chapter, "Apposite Spaces.") These alternatives are all acceptable, although any substitute for a working stone should be crafted from natural materials; avoid plastics, wood-composites, and the like. In the case of formal stone circles, the various elements of the circle including the working stone are oriented in relation to the position of the celestial bodies on auspicious days throughout the year. In the case of simple workings like wand crafting, however, the specific orientation of the elements of the workspace is not important.

Casting

To cast a protective circle, start by sprinkling pure sea salt on the floor or ground in a continuous circle large enough to contain the working stone or work surface and the adept. Leave a gap opposite the working stone (or surface) to facilitate the entry and exit of the adept. Retain a sufficient amount of sea salt to close the gap later in the working; until then, place this salt in a small ceramic bowl at the side of the gap. This sea salt circle with a gap replicates the perimeter stones of a formal stone circle and the entry portal used by the adept. Place candles at each side of the entry portal and light them just before the working begins. Place all the necessary tools, potions, and so forth on the working stone before sealing and cleansing the protective circle. In this particular working, for wand crafting, the adept places a sharp ritual knife and the harvested branch, still within its protective wrapping, onto the working stone together with a lit ritual candle. (The ritual candle is simply a candle dedicated to ritual use, most frequently made from natural ingredients.) The next step is to seal the protective circle.

Sealing

With all of the ritual tools in place, the adept begins the working outside of the protective circle. First, meditate upon the entire working while in a calm, introspective state, repeatedly going over each step of the working in your mind, anticipating any difficulties and arriving at suitable remedies, until the entire working is visualized in its perfect state and clearly fixed within your consciousness. Only then may the adept enter the protective circle, extending each hand to very briefly pass through the purifying flames of the entry portal candles as he passes them. Then, seal the circle using the remaining sea salt while speaking a *sealing intention* similar to the following:

*I seal this protective circle, ensuring all unwanted and
malevolent energies are prevented from entering and that all
within will be protected from any unwelcome influences.*

Cleansing

Once the protective circle has been sealed, the next step is to
cleanse the circle's interior and all that is contained within it. To
do this, face the working stone, raise your hand, and speak a
cleansing intention, such as the following or a similar verbal expression that you have composed:

*Purity is found in its most wholesome form in all aspects of
nature. I call upon this ubiquitous force to cleanse this circle
and all things within it. Remove all unwanted malevolent
energies and purify those energies that remain.*

It is now safe to begin crafting your living wand within the cleansed
circle.

Remove the harvested branch from its protective wrapping and
place it on the working stone. Prepare the cut end of the branch—
the *heel-end*—by cutting away the wax used to seal it with your ritual
knife. Cut about half an inch from the end at an angle of approximately
forty-five degrees. This type of cut allows the core of the branch and its
vital sap to come into direct contact with the adept's hand when the
intention is being cast, as will be shown in chapter seven, "Using Your
Wand."

Next, measure the branch so that its length is equal to the distance between the adept's elbow and the base of the wrist joint, in
other words the length of the arm. Cut the excess branch tip off
with a straight cut. The wand is now ready to be used and it must be
used as soon as possible. As previously discussed, cutting the branch
exposes the wood's vital core and sap to the elements and its spiritual
energy and the potency of its attributes will now begin to deteriorate

and dissipate. Secure the wand in its protective wrapping until it is to be used.

With the crafting working complete, extinguish the candles, erase the salt circle including the entry portal, and collect or disperse the remaining salt. Once used, the salt should not be reused for any future circles.

This completes the crafting and provides the adept with a living wand imbued with the vital attributes and virtues of the chosen tree.

Crafting a Contact Wand

The rudimentary wand created above is ideal for casting intentions at a visible recipient or toward a distant recipient beyond the horizon. It will work equally as well if used to direct an intention toward an object or a space or location. If the desire is to cast an intention through direct contact between the wand and the recipient, however, then the wand must be crafted in a different form, that of the *contact wand*.

The purpose of the contact wand is to act as a conduit, conducting the vital energies from the adept to the recipient by direct contact, closing the gap between them rather than casting the intention across it. In most instances this provides a stronger and more secure contact between the adept and the recipient, thereby reducing any chance of interferences or corruption of the intention in the process. The contact wand is crafted in the same way as the rudimentary wand except both ends of the wand are exposed by cutting away the bark and revealing the sapwood that contains the vital energies of the wood being used.

To craft a contact wand, follow the same steps used to craft a rudimentary wand as explained above. Follow them all the way to the stage of cutting the wand to length. Then, instead of securing the completed wand in its protective wrapping, remove the outer bark from the final one inch lengths at each end of the wand, exposing the inner sapwood at both ends. This produces a wand that has a similar appearance to a stage magician's wand, with the dark bark-covered shaft and the lighter-colored wand tips where the bark has been removed. The purpose of

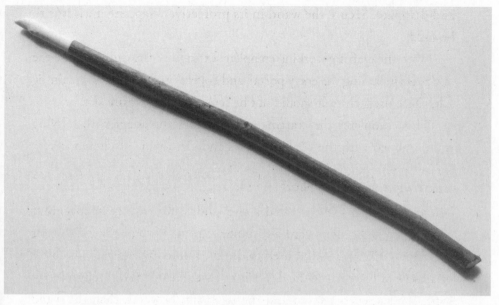

Crafting of a contact living wand, with the contact tip having been stripped of bark.

exposing the inner wood is to allow the exposed heel-end of the wand to be in firm contact with the adept's hand, while the exposed tip of the wand is placed in direct contact with the recipient, closing the "circuit" for the intention to travel directly from one to the other.

A contact wand depends entirely on direct contact between the adept and the recipient. The wand's exposed tip allows the cast energies to broadcast from the end of the wand indiscriminately in every direction in a random, uncontrolled manner. Therefore, a contact wand is not suitable for casting intentions through the air or across any distance.

Both the rudimentary wands and the contact wand are mainstays of the Druids' wands, providing potent, precise, and very focused spiritual energies and utilizing the attributes of whichever tree is chosen in a very specific way.

Other, more complex circumstances may require finely tuned attributes to address complicated situations. Rudimentary wands may be augmented in a number of ways depending upon their intended use. In the following sections we will explore a number of these more complex, sophisticated augmentations along with their intended applications, expanding our understanding of Druidic living wands.

ENTWINED WANDS

Even though nature provides us with trees imbued with a staggering variety of spiritual attributes and virtues, on occasions it may be necessary to enhance or fine-tune these attributes in order to address the needs of more complex circumstances. One of the ways that this may be achieved is by wrapping a rudimentary wand with other, compatible botanicals that then enhance the wand's attributes by imbuing those of its own.

Entwined living wand, bound with freshly harvested ivy.
(See also color plate 3.)

Appropriate Uses for Entwined Wands

The main reasons to craft an *entwined wand* are either to fine-tune the basic rudimentary wand by enhancing its virtues through adding the subtle attributes of another, compatible botanical, or to reduce or eliminate some of the attributes of the original wand by adding other botanicals with contrary attributes that will subdue the unwanted ones. In either case, the entwining botanicals have an influence on the original wand's character. An example of this may be the entwining of mistletoe around an oakwood wand; the mistletoe increases the oak's attributes of wisdom and learning. Another example may be the entwining of ivy around an applewood wand. An applewood wand is generally most effective when directed toward a female recipient; the adept could add ivy, known for its male virtues, in order to use the applewood wand for intentions directed toward a male recipient with more effect.

Choosing Entwining Botanicals

Botanicals chosen for wrapping entwined wands are usually selected because of their propensity to climb and wrap themselves around other plants or objects as they grow. In other words, the plants are being used in a way that harmonizes with their natural growth pattern. Most of these botanicals are found growing on their preferred trees in the wild, often as parasites or while living in a symbiotic relationship with their host. The species of botanical used is chosen primarily because of its own individual attribute(s). *Entwining botanicals* will most often be one of the following four species:

Dog rose: Most frequently used to enhance all intentions related to love and attraction. While a number of wood species share this attribute, this is a virtue that can only benefit from being amplified by dog rose. Ideally used when the plant is flowering, only young, flexible growth lends itself to being entwined around a living wand.

Holly: Enhances any intention requiring the characteristics of peace, security, longevity, and goodwill. A symbol of the evergreen aspect of nature, holly corresponds with wands crafted from species sharing its virtues of lasting commitment, durability, and long life. It is frequently used to balance the deterring virtues of wood species such as the attribute of protection. Holly offsets the banishing aspects of protection with a more subtle "embracing" style of protection.

Ivy: Chosen because of its attributes of bringing things and/or people together. Known for reuniting, sealing relationships, and its powerful binding influence. When entwined around any living wand, ivy will enhance the binding of the intention to the recipient. It is mainly associated with male adepts and intentions directed toward male recipients.

Mistletoe: Probably the most well-known botanical associated with Druidic lore. A prominent element in most images of Druids in the public domain, along with the golden sickle and long white robes, it was a ubiquitous part of the image of the Druidic tradition promoted during the Romantic age. Despite this romanticized propaganda, mistletoe is indeed the most potent botanical in the Druid's repertoire. With its well-established attributes of wisdom, knowledge, purity, integrity, and binding power, mistletoe is used to balance or enhance the properties of almost any wood species used in crafting living wands. Wood species with the attributes of love and affection are, of course, enhanced by mistletoe's virtues of wisdom, purity, and integrity, while mistletoe and sympathetic wood species amplify their shared attribute of binding.

Crafting an Entwined Wand

As with the wood for the original rudimentary wand, all entwining botanicals *must* be identified and harvested in the same manner as the wand branch itself. Take into consideration the species, the botanical's growing environment, all other external influences, and the time of harvesting. All of these factors influence the spiritual energies of the chosen botanical and the effect it has upon the attributes and virtues of the wand as it is used. Like all Druidic living wand components, entwining botanicals must be entwined around the wand as soon as possible after they are harvested to ensure they retain their vital physical and spiritual energies.

To craft an entwined wand, first craft a basic rudimentary wand in exactly the same way as described above. Once the wand has been cut to length, secure the chosen botanical at the wand's heel-end with natural twine. Then twist the botanical carefully around the shaft of the wand in a spiral fashion until it reaches the tip. Secure it there with twine as well. Cut away any remaining botanical so that the end of the botanical is approximately half an inch from the tip of the wand. As a last step, secure the completed entwined wand in its protective wrapping until it is to be used for its casting, which must be as soon as possible after its crafting.

COMPOUND WANDS

Compound wands are the most complex and powerful of all the wand types within Druidic tradition. Each compound wand is constructed from two or more individual wands crafted from separate species of tree as a means of combining their individual attributes into a single potent magical device. As with all Druidic living wands, each of these complex and sophisticated wands is crafted in response to a specific need and engineered so that the compounded influences of the individual component wands may amplify and enhance the intention of the adept.

The simplest form of compound wand is the two-species version, where branches from two separate tree species are interwoven to form a single device. In its most complex form, a compound wand may be constructed from branches harvested from up to six different species of tree and may even include other botanicals to enhance its potential.

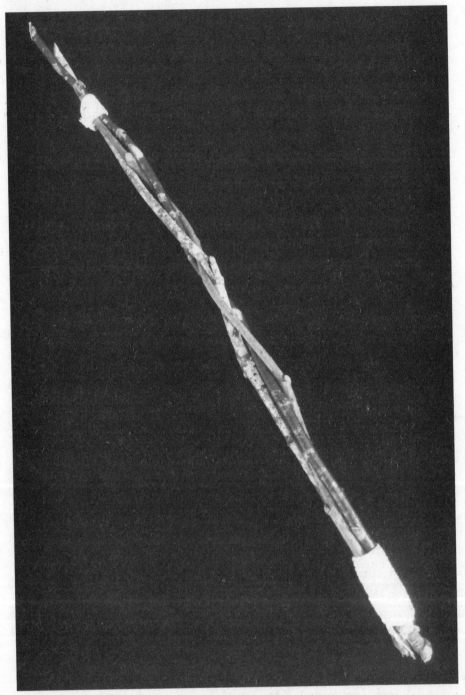

Compound living wand, with individual wands from three complementary tree species. (See also color plate 4.)

Appropriate Uses for Compound Wands

Compound wands are used to cast intentions that cannot be achieved by using the attributes of a single tree species alone. We have seen earlier in this book that each tree species is imbued with particular primary attributes and virtues that are known as its cardinal essences. By combining the individual attributes of any single tree species with those of another species, the adept may craft a living wand that can project attributes not available within a single individual species.

Compound wands may be crafted by combining tree species that share the same or similar attributes in order to amplify and intensify them for a particularly powerful intention. Compound wands may also combine tree species as a means of fine-tuning the attributes and virtues of one of the wood types, for example in response to a very specific need. In each of these instances, the harvested branches of the chosen tree species are plaited, interwoven, or bound together so that when the compound wand is used in a casting, the adept's projected intention is influenced equally by all of the tree species being used. This is why compound wands are so-named—because they *compound* the attributes of each of the tree species being used.

Selecting Wood Combinations for Compound Wands

The first and most important consideration to take into account when selecting which tree species to include in any particular compound wand is what influence each will contribute and exactly how each individual contribution will influence the whole.

Interestingly, according to Druidic lore, by combining or compounding the individual attributes of a number of sources of cardinal essences, in this case a number of tree species, we produce an influence that is greater than the sum of each of the individual parts, a theory that has been attributed to Aristotle and his school of philosophy in ancient Greece. A similar philosophy has been adopted by the Gestalt school of psychological thought in the twentieth century. "The whole is greater than the sum of its parts" has become a widely used expression, and the word *gestalt* is frequently used by a variety of esoteric practitioners, although the concept has been a fundamental aspect of Druidic lore and practice for thousands of years.

With this concept in mind, we can say that crafting a compound wand from just two tree species that display the same or similar attributes will produce a wand with more than twice as much potency as each of the wands would project alone. If more individual wands with similar virtues are added, then the potency of the wand increases exponentially. If, on the other hand, the goal of crafting a compound wand is to dilute the potency of any particular wood species so that the wand may be used in a more nuanced, subtle way, then one or more additional wands with contrary attributes may be interwoven with the first in order to dilute its attributes. It is also possible to use additional wood species to craft a compound wand simply to add attributes not displayed by the first, single wood type.

In summary, compound wands may be crafted from as many types of wood as required to produce the desired combination of attributes. Each individual component wand *must* be chosen and harvested using the same considerations as those employed for the crafting of a single rudimentary wand; this ensures the integrity of each component. Compound wands may be crafted in any one of the following ways:

- By combining two or more wood species with *similar or the same attributes* in order to produce a *more potent* wand.
- By combining two or more wood species with *contradictory attributes* in order to *dilute or refine the attributes* of the wood types.
- By combining two or more wood species with *additional attributes* in order to *augment* the attributes of the wood types.
- By combining two or more wood species with *complementary attributes* in order to *fine-tune* the attributes of the wood types.

In each of these cases, the principle of "the whole is greater than the sum of its parts" is equally applicable.

Augmenting Compound Wands with Additional Botanicals

We have seen previously that various appropriate botanicals—such as ivy, dog rose, or mistletoe—may be entwined around a rudimentary wand to add the botanical's influences to the attributes of the original wood species. In the same way, appropriate botanicals may be included in the crafting of a compound wand to achieve a similar result. We frequently see three- or four-species compound wands augmented with one or more additional botanicals in order to achieve the desired influence.

Review the attributes of the most frequently utilized entwining botanicals outlined above (page 65). Other additional botanicals may be discovered by researching established resources.

Crafting a Compound Wand

To craft a compound wand, begin with the same steps used to craft a rudimentary wand, including casting, sealing, and cleansing a protective circle at the front of a working stone. Remove the harvested branches from their protective wrappings and lay them alongside each other on the working stone so that they are ready for crafting.

To craft a compound wand from two branches, bring them together and tie them with natural twine at the tip-end. Twist the two branches together to form a single shaft, with the bark of both branches touching along their lengths. Then affix them with natural twine near the heel-ends of the branches, at the correct length. Cut the heel-ends of the two branches to form a single diagonal surface that may easily sit in the heel of the adept's hand for casting. Cut the tips of the two branches, which will probably be of different lengths, at a point that creates a length equaling the distance between the adept's elbow and wrist. Then wrap the completed two-shaft compound wand again in its protective cloth until the wand is to be used. Once again, the wand must be used as soon as possible following the crafting, before its vital spiritual energies begin to deteriorate.

To craft a compound wand from more than two branches, bring together however many branches are to be used and tie them with twine at the heel-ends. Plait or interweave the branches along their lengths in a way that brings each branch in touch with the others along the length of their shafts. Then follow the same steps used to craft a two-shaft compound wand: cut the heel-ends to form a single diagonal surface that comfortably sits in the heel of the adept's hand for casting and tie the interwoven branches near the tip before cutting them to a length equaling the distance between the adept's elbow and wrist. Enclose the completed compound wand in its protective wrapping until the wand is to be used.

To augment a compound wand with additional botanicals, interweave the botanicals with the branches as you assemble the compound wand. Secure and cut them in the same way as you would to craft an entwined wand (see above).

RODS

Druidic *rods* may be differentiated from the various wands we have already seen by their length, girth, and purpose. While the length of all wands is defined by the distance from the elbow to the wrist of the adept who crafts and uses it, a rod is crafted to a length equal to the distance from the ground to the waist of the adept. In addition, the girth of a rod should be as close as possible to that of the adept's thumb, giving rise to the rod's alternative name, the *thumb stick*.

Unlike the wand forms we've mentioned, which are meant to accurately direct an intention toward its recipient and are used with a direct *pointing* movement, rods are used to cast more general intentions over a wider location and are used with a sweeping *distribution* movement. For the same reason, the rod is crafted from a thicker branch as it acts as a conduit to a larger, less focused spiritual energy than a shorter wand.

Beyond these points, the rod acts in the same fashion as the living wand, amplifying and enhancing the projected spiritual energies of the adept as it channels and projects his intention toward its intended recipient(s). Like with shorter wands, it is essential that the exposed cross section of the rod branch come into direct contact with the heel of the adept's hand as the intention is cast so that the spiritual energies of the adept can travel through the wand's length, with the intention absorbing the vital attributes of the wand's chosen wood.

Appropriate Uses for Rods

Rods are used in situations in which the intention needs to be spread or distributed over a broad target and is not specifically targeted at an individual recipient. An example may be when an intention is used to cleanse a space or a location, such as a forest grove, a room, or even a stone circle. This cleansing cannot be achieved by a directly focused casting by a shorter living wand, so a living rod is used to distribute the energies of the intention over a wider target area.

Preferred Woods for Rods

The same considerations should be taken into account when choosing the appropriate donor tree species for a rod as in the case of choosing wood for a shorter living wand. A donor tree contains the same attributes and is affected by the same external influences no matter what use it is put to, so the chosen tree species and the specific donor branch contain the same spiritual attributes whether you are selecting them for a shorter living wand or for a rod. The adept should, however, take into account that in casting an intention with a rod, the same attributes and virtues will be distributed over the whole of the wider targeted area and ensure that this is appropriate to everything contained within it.

Crafting a Rod

To begin the crafting, the harvested branch should be sealed at both ends and positioned on the working stone within a sealed and cleansed protective circle, as we have seen above.

Remove the branch from its protective wrapping and cut the heel-end (the end that grew closest to the trunk of the tree) on a diagonal so that it will sit comfortably in the heel of the adept's hand. Placing this end on the ground, mark the branch at a point that is level with the adept's waist. Once the branch is marked, lift it on to the working stone and cut it straight across at the marked length.

Make a shallow cut through the bark only at a distance of two inches from the rod's tip. Remove the bark to expose the internal wood at the tip of the rod. Then, remove the same amount of bark from the heel-end of the rod. This exposes the rod's inner wood at the last two inches of each end while the rest of the shaft remains covered in bark. As a result, the adept's intention will emanate from the entire area of exposed innerwood and not just from the end of the shaft as it does with shorter living wands.

Once you've completed crafting the living rod, enclose in its protective wrapping until it is to be used. Like a wand, a living rod must be used as soon as possible after its crafting. This is even more important with living rods than with shorter living wands because so much of the rod's inner wood is exposed, meaning its living sap will degenerate that much sooner. It has been suggested by many that the appearance of the rod, with its dark shaft and white tips at both ends, gave rise to the image of the magic wand of the stage conjurer or theater magician.

STAFFS

The stereotypical image of the romantic Druid holding a *staff* can still be seen in the majority of publications on Druidic history. Although most of the other aspects of this ubiquitous image are wholly inaccurate, the relationship between the Druid and his or her staff is a lasting legacy of our pagan ancestors. The staff was the first magical device that I was introduced to as a child and it became so much a part of my childhood identity that my nickname was "Stick" throughout my school years and beyond.

Druidic lore tells us that the staff emerged as one of the first tools of ancient folk, who adapted it to almost every imaginable use.

Primarily it was a weapon, a protective device used to both defend against aggressors and wild animals and also to subdue and kill animals for food. When ancient hunter-gatherers settled in extended family groups or clans, the need for foraging and hunting gave way to the growing of crops and the tending of domesticated herds of cattle. In the absence of hunting expeditions and in newly found time to contemplate the spiritual aspects of nature, the role of the staff maintained its protective, defensive reputation and evolved into a spiritual protective device—an *apotropaic device,* giving protection against the curses and malevolent energies that roamed the wild forests and the countryside. Over time, adornments were added to the staff, enhancing its spiritual powers and broadening its potential applications. It became the Druid's inseparable companion, fulfilling an impressive range of needs and desires, and it has maintained its status as a protective device to the present day.

Appropriate Uses for Staffs

Staffs are able to establish secure, shielded spaces and deter or cast away unwanted, harmful energies. The staff's protective energies may be cast forward from its tip, or they may be firmly established by pounding the base of the staff on the ground to "set" or plant a protective intention. The spiritual energies of a staff, either cast or set, are determined in the same way as for all other magical devices—that is, they depend on the internal attributes and virtues of the wood species from which the staff is crafted, tempered by the external influences that affect the donor tree as it grows, just as we have seen with the shorter living wands and the living rod.

Unlike these other wands, however, staffs are typically kept for such a long time that eventually they are no longer *living*. It is very probable that by the end of its useful life a staff may be many years old, with its vital sap degenerated to the point of extinction. This is why almost every staff is augmented with other adornments that amplify the latent energies remaining within the staff as it ages to enhance any and all intentions channeled through the staff itself. Even though the vast majority of the vital sap of the staff may have long since departed, the internal structure of the staff remains intact and functional, meaning that it can still act as a spiritual conduit even when it must depend upon its living adornments to influence any intention it may cast.

Preferred Woods for Staffs

Although the staff may be considered the mainstay of Druidic culture, appearing as it does as the Druid's inseparable companion, it does not rank prominently in the hierarchy of Druidic magical devices. This may be attributed to the fact that it is not truly one of the living devices that the tradition holds so dear. Historically, the staff has always been positioned on the borders of practical implement and magical device, and this remains the case to the present day. As staffs do not depend as heavily on the internal spiritual energies of the wood species they are crafted from, that consideration in the choice of wood species is not as imperative and is frequently compromised for the sake of the wood's durability and strength on a practical basis.

The most popular woods of choice for staffs are oak and hawthorn, mainly because of their powerful attributes in addition to their strength and durability. However, remember that all of the internal and external influences explained previously (in chapter two, "Wood Lore") *must* still be considered when seeking a donor tree. The length of the finished staff should be equal to the height of the adept plus the width across his hand, so the chosen branch must be at least six inches longer than this to allow sufficient wood for the crafting. The girth of a staff branch is determined by the adept but it must be sufficient to create a sturdy, powerful staff with a comfortable handgrip. Ideally, it should be as straight as possible and have as few side branches or sprouting branches growing from it as possible, as these will need to be removed during the harvesting. Cutting a staff branch away from the donor tree may prove very difficult with the ritual knife, so a clean, purified wood saw may be used instead.

Crafting a Staff

As with the other magical devices we have seen above, crafting a staff begins with removing the harvested branch from its protective wrapping and positioning it on the working stone within a sealed and cleansed protective circle. The base of the staff is identified—this will be the cut end that grew closest to the donor tree's trunk—and then it is cut cleanly across about two inches from the end, to remove its sealing wax and produce a flat, firm base. Then the length of the staff is measured and marked. The length, again, should be equal to the height of the adept plus the width of his hand. Then the staff branch is cut cleanly across at the marked point to produce the tip of the staff.

Trim the cut edges of the staff's base and tip with a knife to form a beveled edge (a smooth, sloping edge around the circumference of the staff) and remove the bark from the last two inches of both ends to expose the inner wood. The staff is now complete and ready for use. Many adepts adopt the completed staff as their companion for a period of up to a year so that a spiritual understanding and bond may develop between them before adding any of the augmentations and adornments that elevate the staff to the level of a magical device.

Staff Adornments

As a staff ages its vital sap degenerates and its spiritual energies dissipate. As a result, the adept becomes more attuned to the staff at the same time that its internal attributes diminish. As this is a well-known and accepted process, there comes a point where the probationary (newly or recently crafted) staff must be elevated to the level of a potent magical device. After the crafting, this is done through a second ritual working (called the elevation working) in which the adept secures carefully chosen adornments to the staff so that their attributes may permeate the staff and influence any intentions cast through it.

Typical staff adornments may include:

- Twigs or small branches newly harvested from selected tree species, with or without leaves attached
- Nuts of selected species, freshly harvested and tied in bunches or contained in potion bags
- Seeds of selected species, freshly harvested and contained in potion bags
- Bunches of berries from selected species, freshly harvested
- Bird feathers newly shed from selected species
- Snake skins newly shed from selected species
- Plant roots freshly dug from selected species
- Bark freshly cut from selected species
- Thorns freshly harvested from the briar and contained in potion bags or potion bottles
- Thistles, freshly harvested and tied in bunches or contained in potion bags
- Flower heads newly harvested from selected species, tied in bunches or contained in potion bags
- Specially crafted liquid or powder potions in sealed potion bottles
- Newly abandoned nests of selected species of bird
- Written intentions/incantations on parchment or bark contained in potion bags
- Any combination of the above items

For items described as *freshly harvested, freshly dug, freshly shed,* and so on, this means that they have a known provenance, are used within a few hours of being harvested, and that they are to be returned to nature once the intended working or ritual is complete (see chapter 8, "Returning Your Wand to Nature). All liquid potions and powder potions are crafted and all other adornments are bundled or tied, cleansed, and prepared prior to conducting the elevation working.

The Elevation Working

The *elevation working* is used to add adornments to a staff, thereby elevating it to the level of a magical device. This working, like the others, should be conducted within a sealed and cleansed protective circle, with the chosen adornments positioned along with the staff on the adept's working stone to begin. Often the adept will have carved his most auspicious magic emblems and marks into the staff during its "probationary" period, removing the outer bark to create whatever patterns and marks are most significant to him in preparation for the elevation working.

To complete the elevation working, use natural twine to fix or tie the prepared staff adornments, chosen for their individual and combined attributes, to points along the shaft of the staff in the preferred locations of the adept, about a quarter of the way down from the tip of the staff.

Once the adornments have been attached to the staff it is ready to be used for the working or ritual for which it was crafted. Typically more than one staff adornment is used, and the chosen adornments are selected to uniquely influence the channeled intention of the adept in order to address the specific and individual needs of a particular circumstance. Once the adorned staff's purpose is achieved, the adornments are removed and returned to nature. Without its adornments, the staff returns to its more practical personality with the limited spiritual energies of an aged wood. It is important to mention here that Druidic staffs are never embellished or adorned with embedded crystals, stones, or other inanimate objects, nor do they project piercing beams of light into darkness or fill castle courtyards with glowing mist—no matter how impressive these feats may appear on the cinema screen.

CURIOUS WANDS

While the various wands we have seen above will allow the adept to address most of the many circumstances that might arise, there are occasions when more unusual types of wands may be more suitable. In order to obtain a full understanding of Druidic living wands it is necessary to explore some of these less obvious and less well-known wands and some of the materials from which they are crafted.

Hook Wand

The *hook wand* is used exclusively in attraction workings. It may be crafted from any tree species that has the attributes of attraction, love, or wealth. The wand is crafted from a single branch with a secondary smaller branch sprouting at its base. The longer main branch becomes the principal shaft of the wand, while the sprouting secondary branch is cut shorter to form the hook. The wand is used in the opposite direction as all other wands; the tip of the wand is at the nearest point to the tree's trunk, where the hook is, and its heel-end is the growing end, the end of the longer branch. When being used, the wand is held at the end of the longest shaft, with the shorter branch closest to the targeted person or object. With the hook shape facing the adept, he may hook his target, drawing the person or object toward himself.

The selection of the tree species for a hook wand and the principles underpinning the harvest are the same as with all other wands, as are the methods used in its crafting, which takes place at the working stone, sealed within a protective circle. The first stage of crafting begins with cutting the tip-end of the main shaft at a point approximately one inch beyond the junction where the sprouting secondary branch emerges. This becomes the projection point of the wand, the point where the influence is projected toward its recipient, as with the standard rudimentary wand we have seen before. The secondary "hook" branch is then cut to a length of approximately three inches. Finally, the heel-end of the main shaft is cut to a length that equals the distance from the adept's elbow to his wrist. It must be cut diagonally so that it sits comfortably in the heel of the adept's hand for casting. This completes the crafting of the hook wand and, as always, it must be used as soon as possible after its crafting, before its vital energies begin to dissipate.

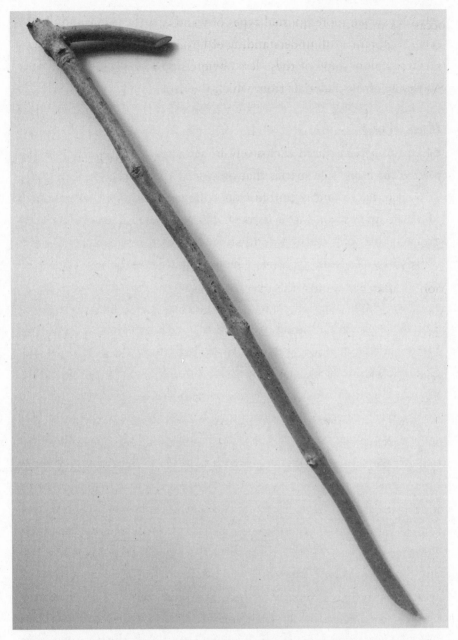

Hook living wand, used for attraction workings.

Casting with a hook wand is a two-step process. The first is to cast the intention in the normal way by pointing and projecting (this process will be explained in detail in chapter seven, "Using Your Wand"). The second step is to immediately move the wand in a hooking action to attract the recipient, object, or emotion to the adept. If the adept is acting as an intermediary, as with attracting a loving emotion from an individual and then projecting it toward a third party, this must be undertaken immediately to be effective. To do this, the adept must point and project the intention toward the third party immediately following the hooking movement.

There is a second type of hook wand, made from the thorny branch of a blackberry bush, that is used to attract unwanted, malevolent energies and then cast them aside in a way similar to an exorcism. This is explained in detail in the next section on thorn wands.

Thorn Wand

The *thorn wand* is unusual in that it is not crafted from a donor tree species but from a harvested thorn briar branch (the thorny branch of a bramble, or blackberry, bush). In choosing the appropriate thorn branch, all the considerations we have seen previously—regarding location, terroir, external influences, and harvesting times—apply in the same way as with other wands, even though the briar is classified as a

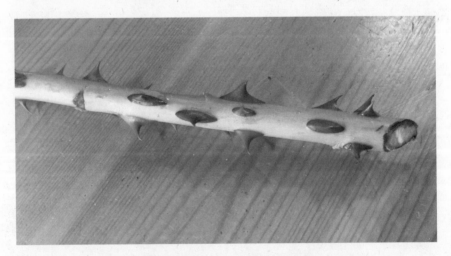

Rudimentary thorn living wand with its thorns intact.
(See also color plate 5.)

bush and not a tree. Depending upon the season in which the branch is harvested it may be adorned with its new leaves, flowers, or berries, but it is essential that it is covered in a strong and healthy array of thorns. Wands crafted from thorn briar have the attributes of power, intensity, protection, aggression, and security.

Thorn wands are crafted in three different forms, each with its own specific purpose. The *rudimentary thorn wand* is a typical rudimentary wand but one that projects the attributes defined by the many individual thorns along its shaft.

The *hook thorn wand* is a hook wand similar to the one described previously. It is crafted like a rudimentary thorn wand but with the thorns removed—except for a single thorn left at the tip of the shaft to act as the hook.

Thorn wands can be part of a *protective deposit bundle*—five or seven short (four to six inch) wands tied in a bundle and deposited in a particular place as a protective (apotropaic) device to defend against unwanted malevolent energies. Thorny briar branches are excellent to

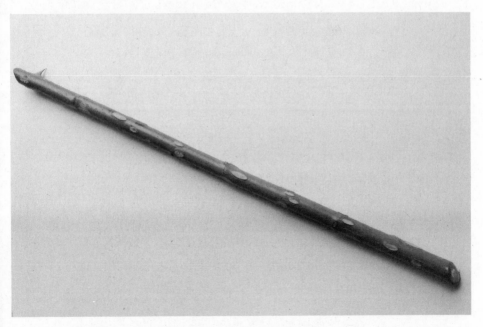

Hook thorn living wand with one "hooking" thorn left at the tip.

Protective deposit bundle, which includes a thorn wand.

use in protective deposit bundles because of their protective attributes (see "Protective Bundles and Protective Wands" on page 91).

Each of these versions of thorn living wands share the same protective attributes. Although they may be used in a variety of different ways, they all illustrate the defensive and apotropaic attributes of the thorn. As with all living wands, each is crafted at the working stone within a sealed and cleansed protective circle.

To craft a rudimentary thorn wand, the heel of the wand, the end nearest the root or main trunk, is cut at a diagonal, as per usual, to sit comfortably within the heel of the adept's hand for casting. The briar branch is then measured and marked at a point equal to the distance from the adept's elbow to his wrist and any excess is cut away. The crafting of the rudimentary thorn wand now complete, the wand is secured in its protective wrapping and used as soon as possible, before its vital energies begin to dissipate. The rudimentary thorn wand is used in casting the working in the normal way. (For more on casting, see chapter seven, "Using Your Wand.")

To craft a hook thorn wand, the first step is to cut the heel-end at a diagonal in the usual way. The branch is then measured to a length equal to the distance between the adept's elbow and his wrist and any excess is cut away. The strongest single thorn near the tip is then identified and all other thorns along the length of the shaft are carefully removed by pushing them with the thumb at a ninety-degree angle to the shaft. The thorns should come away from the shaft with the least possible damage to the branch (as well as to the adept's hand), leaving only a small "cup groove" on the branch in place of the thorn. The wand is now complete with the de-thorned wand shaft and a single "hooking" thorn near its tip. The hook thorn living wand is used in exactly the same way as the hook wand, with first a pointing projection and then a hooking action.

Forked Wand

The Druidic *forked wand* is a Y-shaped living wand, most frequently crafted from either wych elm or willow wood. Willow has a close association with water and has the added attributes of divination and revelation. A parallel may be drawn between the forked wand and the divining rod or witching rod of the ancient cunning folk community (those such as witches, sorcerers, herbal healers, and Druids knowledgeable about the spiritual and physical benefits of botanicals and their related workings) or the dowsing/divining rods used by modern-day dowsers to locate hidden water sources. Many belief systems around the world employ similar devices to search for underground water sources, metal deposits, gemstone deposits, or even to rediscover lost burial sites. Over millennia, such magical devices have been used to determine and locate the spiritual energies held within the Earth, energies that more recently have been described as ley lines or power lines, which join auspicious sites or energy deposits lying beneath the Earth's surface. The common factor linking all of these interpretations is the wand or rod's ability to identify and locate sources of energy within the Earth without the use of scientific equipment. These invisible forces may be emitted by a natural, physical deposit of water, metal, gemstones, oil, and so on, or they may be the source of a spiritual energy that the adept seeks to attune to or utilize.

In the Druidic tradition, such forked wands are used in two ways. The first is as a dowsing wand and the second is as a *listening wand*. Each wand is crafted from either the wood of the wych elm or the willow tree—their common aspect is their affinity with water and the natural landscape. Both are way-finding trees and have traditionally been employed as markers in the landscape for travelers and as a means of tying spiritual energies to a specific location.

The forked wand is harvested from a location within the selected donor tree's canopy from a point where a single branch divides into two, forming the distinctive Y shape that defines the wand's characteristics. The donor tree and the specific branch group are chosen and harvested by taking into account all of the considerations we have seen with the other living wands. Following its harvesting the branch group's cut ends are sealed with wax to retain the wood's vital sap and spiritual energies before being carefully covered in its protective wrapping until it is to be crafted and used. In some instances, only the single, main shaft is cut from the donor tree and the other two branches that form the Y shape are left uncut until the wand is crafted. In other instances, if the two branches that form the Y shape are too long to remain until the crafting takes place, it may be necessary to cut all three branches as the wand is harvested. It is important that all three branches are of the same thickness and length as each other.

As above, the forked wand is crafted at a working stone within a sealed, cleansed protective circle. Unlike other wands, all three branch ends are cut straight across; there is no need to cut at a diagonal as the wand is not used in the same way as the others. To craft a forked wand, the first step is to cut the single main branch to a length equal to the distance from the adept's elbow to his wrist. Following this, the other two branches are cut to the same length in the same way; in other words, measuring from the junction of the Y to the growing ends of the shorter branches, each of those lengths should also be equal to the distance between the adept's elbow and wrist. With this, the crafting of the forked wand is complete, and the wand is returned to its protective wrapping until it is to be used.

The forked wand is unique within the Druidic tradition because it is used to *collect* spiritual energy instead of to project it. Most frequently, forked wands are used to detect spiritual energy and identify the locations where these energies are most powerful. This is achieved in one of two ways. The first way is to hold the two branches that form the Y shape and use the single main branch as a conduit or receptor, where the strength of the spiritual energy is interpreted by the adept.

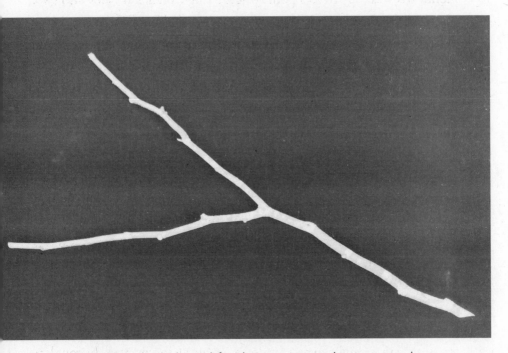

Forked living wand, used for divining or as a listening wand.

The second way is to place the ears to the edges of the two secondary branches and, again using the single main branch as a receptor, the adept experiences the changes in spiritual energy by "hearing" the otherwise silent radiation of spiritual energy and assessing its strength accordingly. *Warning:* It is important to emphasize that the adept *must never* place the ends of the forked branches *into* his or her ears. *Doing so is extremely dangerous.* Instead, the adept "listens" to the wand's response along the length of the two branches that form the Y shape by placing them carefully *against* the ears.

Within the Druidic oral tradition there are accounts of influential Druids identifying auspicious forest groves and other important locations by using one or another of these techniques. Stories tell of standing stones and stone circles being erected at locations that were divined in one of these ways. This proposition helps explain the locations of many stone circles even though other more practical locations may seem like they would have been more suitable. On this point, it is worth considering this theory in a little more depth here.

Location of Stone Circles, Standing Stones, and Other Auspicious Locations

At first sight, it may seem peculiar that many stone circles are located in such inconvenient places when we know that they served as regular ritual places and daily assembly places for Druids in their communities. Why, for example, are many stone circles not located next to convenient sources of water or alongside arable fields? We find convincing evidence that stone circles were surrounded by huts and living spaces together with all the other aspects of the everyday life of their communities, even though the people living in these villages may have had to carry water for miles or up steep hills to reach their homes.

The obvious explanation for this is that the first priority of the nomadic people who settled in these villages was not the convenience of the necessary resources they needed to survive, but the location of the stone circle that was at the heart of their ancient culture. In other words, the first and most important

The stone circle near the town of Kenmare in County Kerry, Ireland. (See also color plate 6.)

factor of where the villagers settled was the correct placement of the stone circle they were to build, and only once this location had been determined would they settle, build the stone circle, and construct the huts and living spaces around it. Water access, suitable arable land, good grazing land for their cattle, and other necessities were secondary to the spiritual imperatives of these communities. This theory contradicts the many long-standing beliefs that suggest that our ancestors built their stone circles conveniently close to the villages in which they settled. Now there is widespread recent archaeological evidence that tells us that the stone circles were built first, with the circles' builders constructing their huts around the sites of the circles and then expanding the settlements into villages as the members of the builders' extended families joined them in their work. We must then accept that these ancient builders shared the beliefs of the learned Druids in their communities, built the stone circles at the location the Druids determined, and constructed them according to their instruction. Only once this was done did the communities settle around these places of ritual.

We can also see that this process was not undertaken without sophisticated consideration. As mentioned, in many cases, preliminary wooden stakes were used to confirm the positioning prior to the erection of the huge upright stones that make up the circles we still see in our landscape some five thousand years later. With the exact location of each standing stone in the stone circles being so important, we can understand how essential it must have been for the Druids to identify their positions correctly. This was done in exactly the same way as it is today, by using the same key considerations to determine the exact locations and orientations of the stones in the circle before erecting them. While significant features in the surrounding landscape and elevation are important to determining these details, the most critical factor is the spiritual energy emanating from the location of the circle.

This was determined using the magical device we have just explored—the forked wand, specifically the listening wand. Spiritual energy identified in this manner determined the location of many, if not all, of the stone circles that remain, along with the many stone circles that have disappeared beneath the towns and cities we live in today.

Protective Bundles and Protective Wands

For thousands of years our ancestors depended upon the learned Druids that served their communities to protect them from what they understood to be the many unwanted malevolent spiritual energies that threatened them in their everyday life. Very often, this protection would be accomplished through the combined use of potions, amulets, charms, counter-curses, intentions, and apotropaic devices carefully deposited in order to keep unwanted energies at bay. Many of our museums have within them artifacts that are known to be protective devices discovered in places as diverse as chimneys, barns, gateways, and attics, appearing to have been placed there hundreds if not thousands of years ago. The protective devices themselves are as diverse as their locations and include desiccated cat remains, shoes, potion bottles, horse skulls, curse dolls, and caches made up of collections of what may best be called *meaningful objects*. While the current understanding is that many of these artifacts were deposited as part of a folk magic tradition that we now think of as witchcraft, it is also accepted that these traditions find their roots in the much older folk magic of the rural cunning folk and the Druids of the pre-Celtic era.

Among these ancient protective devices was (and still is) the Druidic protective deposit bundle, which often includes thorn wands, as touched on earlier in this chapter. These bundles of either five or seven short, four to six inch wands are crafted using carefully chosen wood types that are known to have distinctive protective and banishing attributes.

The choice of wood species is determined by the bundle's eventual application and may include a mixture of species with protective attributes, some with the attribute of longevity (to prolong the bundle's effectiveness), others with the ability to amplify these attributes, and yet others that can dilute the potency of invading energies. The bundles are placed in vulnerable locations (such as doorways, windows, chimney breasts, gates, and entry passageways) where it is thought that malevolent energies may invade a home, farm building, field, or forest grove.

The crafting of protective deposit bundles is undertaken at a working stone within a sealed, cleansed protective circle. The crafting begins with the five or seven short wands being laid out in a row on the working stone. The sealed end of each wand is cut to reveal its inner vital core. Each is then measured to the same length, between 4 and 6 inches, and the excess trimmings retained to be returned to nature as explained later. The short wands are then assembled into a bundle with thorns and spiked leaves on the outside. The bundle is tied securely at both ends using natural twine. Like all living wands, the completed bundle is then carefully returned to its protective wrapping until it is to be deposited (see "Using Apotropaic Bundles," page 151).

In addition to these potent apotropaic bundles, Druidic lore also utilizes the inherent protective energies of individual wood types to craft individual *protective wands*. Crafting such protective wands forms an imperative part of the repertoire of every Druidic adept.

The donor tree or plant for each living protective wand is identified and harvested using exactly the same criteria as we have seen above, with consideration of the protective attributes of the species tempered by the external influences that the tree has been exposed to. The most frequently chosen species include the holly tree and the bramble (blackberry), which both demonstrate their protective attributes through their role in nature, where they protect themselves from being grazed by animals with their defensive spikey leaves and thorns. Both of these plants may be crafted into wands with their leaves and thorns left intact along their shafts or with the thorns and leaves removed apart from at the

A typical collection of branches from protective tree species used to craft a living protective bundle. (See also color plate 7.)

A protective deposit bundle with a combination of complementary protective wood species. (See also color plate 8.)

tip. In the latter case, the thorns and leaves remain near the ends of the wands in order to intensify the channeled projection. An odd number of thorns (or spiky leaves) is always retained, typically three or five, depending on the adept's intuition. Protective living wands may also be entwined with additional botanicals such as nettle or dog rose to enhance their protective characteristics.

Binding Bundles

Another form of bundle made up of small wands from a variety of wood species is the *binding bundle*. Binding bundles are crafted from even smaller wand branches and given during a binding working as a means of strengthening the bond between the individuals or objects being bound together by the ritual. The bundles contain any number of individual small wands, each approximately three inches in length. The donor tree species are chosen for their intrinsic attributes and combined to complement the intended outcome as a whole. The following example describes crafting a binding bundle to enhance a love binding working between two individuals.

The adept has chosen to include wand branches from four tree species: oak, for strength and longevity; hazel, for potency; dog rose, for love and affection; and yew, for wisdom. A short, six-inch branch is cut from each of the donor trees, each having been identified using the same criteria as we have seen above. The cut ends of each branch are sealed and then they are all are secured in protective wrapping until the bundle is to be crafted.

The crafting of the bundle is undertaken within a sealed, cleansed protective circle. The individual short wands are arranged in a row on the working stone. The sealed end of each is cut across to expose the wood's vital inner core. Each is then cut to a length of three inches in order to form a consistent contribution of attributes from all the short wands being used. All the short wands are then brought together to form the bundle and are then tied firmly with natural twine. If any additional botanicals are to be added to enhance the bundle, these are interwoven before the bundle is bound. The crafting of the binding bundle is now complete, and it is secured in its protective wrapping until it is to be used.

Binding bundles of this kind are frequently given as a token for enhancing a binding ritual such as a handfasting or betrothal. Flower posies, or nosegays, assembled from flowers selected for their same attributes of attraction and binding, a pagan tradition also used by Druids in a similar way to assembling binding bundles with living branches, may indeed have been the forerunner of the modern bridal bouquet. Binding bundles are usually kept by the recipient to ensure the chosen attributes continue to have the intended effect.

In a more clandestine way, binding bundles may also be crafted and empowered in secret. These bundles are sometimes placed under the pillow, in the clothing, or close to the intended recipient so that its influence may act upon the recipient without his or her knowledge.

Crafted binding bundle with a combination of living wands from complementary binding tree species.

Such bundles might be used to stop an unfaithful partner from straying or to attract and bind the attention of a desired love.

Brewing Wands and Rods

Brewing wands are yet another form of living wand crafted for a very specific use. One of the things that the ancient Druids proved to be very proficient at was the brewing of ales, ciders, meads, and metheglyn, an activity they shared with the cunning folk and brew-wives (also known as alewives or brewsters) of their rural communities. Each Druid had his own recipes and, as hops were not an indigenous plant, they were obliged to include various other bittering agents as an alternative. These bittering agents were included to counteract the sweetness of the honey and other sugar sources necessary to produce the required fermentation and alcohol production. They were often botanicals that had their own psychotropic effects and on occasion the influence of the psychotropic plants had a greater effect than the alcohol they were combined with. The majority of these fermented brews were intended to be used in a social drinking function and as an alternative to water, as fresh, unpolluted drinking water was often scarce. Some were taken during group rituals, others simply as a form of relaxation. Of those most often brewed by the Druid, by far the majority were crafted as a means of aiding the ingestion of the physical healing properties of the botanicals they were fermented with and the absorption of the spiritual attributes of the carefully selected herbs, flowers, barks, and roots that were macerated in the fermenting brew.

The most popular of the fermented Druidic brews was (and still is) mead. Fermented from wild honey and water, mead is widely acknowledged as one of the first alcoholic drinks known to humankind. It is possible it was first discovered when wild honey, stored for the winter season, became infected with wild, airborne yeast and fermented to form an alcoholic liquid that soon became recognized for its relaxing and "feel-good" effect. Over time, again possibly as a result of winter storage gone awry, it was discovered that the same alcoholic liquid (mead) was an effective preservative and would assimilate the curative properties, both physical and spiritual, of any botanical macerated in it. This curative combination of botanicals macerated in the fermenting mead became known as *metheglyn,* from the Welsh, meaning "medicinal wine." Although both mead and its more complex partner metheglyn became well established in history and within the Druidic tradition, as we may expect there was no understanding of the science underpinning the fermentation process and the way that the sugars contained in the honey and assorted plants were converted into alcohol in the presence of a yeast. Nor did the Druids understand that this yeast—such an essential component in the fermentation process—was both airborne and thrived on the surface and inner parts of the vegetables, herbs, and so on that they used in their everyday life. Instead, they thought the fermentation process was a random, spiritual phenomenon, produced by nature to benefit humankind. With no understanding of the principles involved, it was impossible for them to know why some batches of stored honey fermented into mead while others remained in their natural harvested state. The one thing they did understand, however, was that when the Druid diluted their honey with water and stirred it with their magical wand, it *always* turned into mead, so the secret catalyst to begin the process was the Druid's wand. And so, the Druid's *brewing wand* became an established and essential element of the crafting of mead.

The brewing wand appeared to remove the random element from the mead brewing process and to significantly increase the probability of the honey being converted into mead. This is the function of the Druid's brewing wand that is contained in the oral tradition of the Druids of South Wales. Though in times past no scientific explanation was offered to support this theory, today's teaching often explores the physical elements of fermentation, though no one has yet been able to describe the spiritual elements in a way that reconciles with today's science. It is suggested that as the Druid's brewing wand is normally used for a whole brewing season without being washed, since it is felt that washing any wand once it had been crafted and empowered removes many of its spiritual characteristics, the naturally occurring wild yeast on the bark of the new wand is transferred to the brew, and that the yeast culture developing on the surface of the brewing wand increases after every use and kick-starts the fermentation process within the honey-water solution. While there is no doubt that airborne wild yeast also contributes to the fermentation process, there is a sound scientific argument that the brewing wand itself is indeed a major source of yeast.

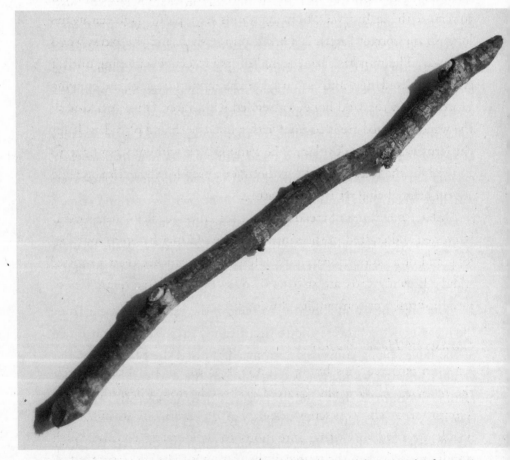

Oak brewing wand, used to invigorate a fermenting brew and infuse it with the essential attributes of the oak tree.

The Druid's brewing wand is always crafted from an oak tree branch. The donor tree and the individual branch are chosen and harvested using the same criteria we have seen with the other living wands described above. The cut end(s) are sealed, and the harvested branch is secured in a protective wrapping until it is to be crafted. In this instance, it is even more obvious that the branch must be crafted and used as soon as possible after it is harvested to maintain the spiritual energies of its sap core and the physical properties of its surface bark, as these attributes are to be conveyed in the brew.

The brewing wand is crafted within a sealed, cleansed protective circle. It is removed from its protective wrapping and the heel-end is cut to remove the sealing wax. Brewing wands are typically eighteen inches long, so the correct length is marked on the shaft and the excess wood cut away. The wand is then secured in its protective wrapping until it is needed. Brewing wands are used at the mixing stage of the brewing process, when the wild honey is blended with water. Once stirred with the wand, the mixture is covered with a linen cloth and placed aside for the fermentation to take place. The wand is kept, without washing it, to be used for the next brew and will often be used for the entire brewing season before being returned to nature.

If large quantities of mead are to be mixed, a sturdier *brewing rod* is harvested and crafted in the same way. The rod may be up to four feet long and of a proportionate circumference (i.e. thicker than a shorter wand). Brewing rods are still used today to brew large quantities of mead for ritual or community consumption.

Corkscrew Hazel Wands

An even more curious living wand crafted for a very specific use is the *corkscrew hazel wand*. Crafted exclusively from *Corylus avellana* 'Contorta,' or the corkscrew hazel plant (a deciduous shrub), these wands are used in casting intentions to deliberately confuse. Such wands are used when the source of the casting is to be kept secret, when the goal is to cause confusion in anyone trying to cast a counter-casting,

Corkscrew hazel living wand, with the fresh leaves
removed from the shaft.

or when a secret curse is to be cast. Corkscrew hazel wands introduce confusion and chaos. They are used in only the most secret castings and the most profound curses. Very few Druids will even admit to their existence, let alone explain their use.

The first thing we notice when we observe corkscrew hazel is the twisted, tangled formation of its branches, each growing in what appears to be ever-changing, random directions. The shape of the plant's branches give the shrub its common name. Corkscrew hazel is relatively rare and can be difficult to find. Usually growing to a height of around five feet, the shrub is very distinctive and easy to identify owing to its contorted branch formations. Once a donor is found, the harvesting is undertaken with consideration of all the usual criteria. Very few of the branches of the corkscrew hazel grow to substantial size, so it may well be that the harvested branch is thinner and lighter than the wand branches of other species This will be compensated for, however, by the complexity of the branch itself. Since the branch is to be crafted into a conduit to channel the confusion-inducing intention of the adept, it is important to choose the branch with the most complex, contorted growth pattern. This is because as the cast intention channels its way through the wand, the pattern of confusion and chaos will be imprinted upon it by the contorted wand branch.

The crafting of a corkscrew hazel wand should be undertaken within a sealed, cleansed protective circle. The heel-end of the wand is cut across at a diagonal to remove the sealing wax and produce effective contact with the heel of the hand of the adept during the casting. The length of the wand is variable as it is not usual for the tip to not be cut but instead be left intact, often with a small number of leaves still attached. After the crafting, the completed wand is then secured in its protective wrapping, while taking care to keep all its twisted corkscrew elements intact even if its structure is thin, delicate, and fragile. As with other living wands, all corkscrew hazel wands *must* be used as soon as possible after crafting in order to maintain their vital spiritual energies and attributes.

Flying Staffs

Although not truly a wand, *flying staffs* are harvested and crafted in the same way as wands, though they are used in a more practical, if not surprising, way. Possibly the forerunner of the well-known witch's broom, the flying staff is, like the witch's broom, used as a means of magical or spiritual transportation within the mundane world. While it may be more than a little far-fetched to imagine the skies filled with witches and Druids riding their brooms and staffs, flitting from one destination to the next, it is entirely feasible that adepts may be spiritually transported using devices such as the flying staff.

Many cultures have a tradition of magic adepts transporting themselves by riding a variety of common, everyday items like brooms or carpets, elevating these well-known simple household articles from their mundane function to the level of magical devices under the control of the adept who commands them. Though many of these traditional stories may sound unbelievable and as if they were designed to entertain young children at bedtime, like many other folk tales, they have their foundations in the ancient lore of the cultures in which they developed. Indeed, many have their origins in the practical, mystical beliefs of generations past. This is very much the case with most "flying" traditions.

Many Eastern traditions maintain the concept of spiritual travel portrayed in a more understandable form, within tales of flying carpet journeys or riding atop mythical birds, dragons, or other fantastical beasts. Although many of these tales describe physical journeys, they disguise the fact that the teller of these tales often uses them as a metaphor for the much less understood concept of spiritual travel, or what may now be known as transcendental travel. It is not unusual for the term transcendental travel to be closely associated with both meditation and the use of psychoactive substances, each used to induce a state of mind expansion, elevated consciousness, and otherworldliness. All of these concepts were well known to our ancestors and in particular to the ancient adepts such as the Druids of Northern Europe and the British Isles.

The use of psychotropic botanicals has been well established within Druidic lore since time immemorial, as has the practice of calming meditation. It is this combination of mind elevating botanicals and deep meditation that explains the use of flying staffs and, of course, the witch's broom and gives insight into the part each plays in spiritual transportation. For use with flying staffs, the psychotropic botanicals are crafted into an ointment, known as *flying ointment*. The ointment is intended to be applied to the body so that the active ingredients are absorbed through the skin, a process known as *transdermal absorption*. In crafting flying ointment, the chosen psychotropic herbs and barks are pummeled together in a mortar and pestle to release their active ingredients. The resultant paste is then pummeled further with the

A witch's broom, a possible version of the Druidic flying staff.
(See also color plate 9.)

adept's choice of natural fat—usually vixen or roe deer—to combine the ingredients. The ointment is usually crafted in the adept's workshop and stored in their general cache. If it is not crafted within a protective circle, then it must be cleansed before it is used.

Warning!

The crafting and use of flying ointment should never be undertaken lightly. Both require an in-depth knowledge and understanding of the use of a range of herbs and barks that, if misused or misidentified, could and likely will cause serious harm or even death.

The flying staff is normally around four feet long, a convenient length to allow for manipulation by the user during the spiritual flying ritual. Flying staffs are most often crafted from the wood of the rowan tree, a tree well known to witchcraft as we have discussed above. To craft a flying staff, the donor branch (at least four feet long) is chosen and harvested in the same way and using the same selective criteria as we have seen previously for crafting living wands. The flying staff's intended use means that it must be of a reasonable thickness in proportion to its length; therefore, it is highly likely that it will be harvested from a mature rowan tree with sturdy side branches. The harvested branch is sealed at its cut end and secured in its protective wrapping until it is to be crafted.

Ideally, the flying staff is crafted within the confines of a sealed, cleansed protective circle. It is first removed from its wrapping and laid on the working stone. The heel-end of the branch is then cut, removing the sealing wax and exposing the wood's vital inner core. The tip of the staff, the end growing furthest from the trunk of the donor tree, is then cut to create a finished staff approximately four feet in length. The excess wood is retained to be returned to nature when the working is complete. The staff's bark is then removed from the final nine inches of the shaft at both ends, in order to expose the inner wood. These areas are then trimmed to form a smooth surface by removing any unwanted growth. The exposed tip-end of the staff is the section where the flying ointment is to be applied, while the heel-end is gripped firmly by the adept when casting the accompanying intention, thereby making a firm unbroken connection between the adept and the focal point of the channeling (the staff). After crafting, the flying staff is then secured in its protective wrapping until it is to be used, which must be as soon as possible to ensure the integrity of its spiritual energies.

Feathers as Wands

In addition to the more well-known botanical wands, there are a few other organic materials that can be used as wands. One of these alternatives is bird feathers. Feathers are grouped with wands here due to a number of common factors: They retain the vital attributes of the donor birds they are collected from, just like different woods retain the attributes of specific donor trees. *Feathers used as living wands* are crafted and utilized while they still retain their vital spiritual energies. This means living feathers wands must be used as soon as possible after the feathers are obtained. Feathers are only effective as wands when they are of known provenance. They should be from a specific bird, taking into account all the same criteria that apply to crafting with wood and other botanicals. Most important of these considerations is the source of the individual feather.

As with botanicals, each species of bird is imbued with its own characteristic attributes that may be used to enhance and amplify an intention that is channeled through a living feather wand. In the particular example we shall explore, a collared-dove wing feather is used to demonstrate the overarching principles in crafting and using feathers as wands. The collared-dove is indigenous to the British Isles and is therefore well known within the Druidic tradition. Its virtues and attributes include its ability to amplify any casting related to love, affection,

Crow and dove feathers to be used as living feather wands.

attraction, or binding, and it enhances the adept's intention so that it can be cast over the horizon and to locations and recipients such as forest groves, distant homes, and individuals living far away from where the intention is being cast. Using a feather wand in this way enables the adept to influence places and people at a distance while eliminating the need for spiritual journeying.

Harvesting a feather may be as simple as observing a bird until it sheds a wing feather and collecting it or as potentially difficult as capturing the bird and removing a feather before releasing the bird again. It should be said that if done responsibly while treating the bird with care and respect, carefully removing a single wing feather causes no lasting harm to the bird as many birds often lose or shed feathers on a regular basis. When they lose a single wing feather, many birds will themselves remove a similar feather from their other wing to rebalance their flight characteristics, but this of course must be the choice of the bird. However the feather is collected, it must be newly removed or shed by the bird so that any external influences like weather, season, location, and so forth may be taken into consideration, just as in the case of crafting botanical wands. The collected feather is then carefully secured in a protective wrapping until it is to be crafted and used, which must be as soon as possible following its collection.

The structure of the feather, particularly its hollow shaft, make it ideal as a channel for projecting the adept's intentions and enabling its own attributes to enhance the intention as it flows through its shaft. When using a feather as a wand, it is held at its shaft end and the feathered tip is pointed toward the intention's recipient. The feather is crafted into a wand at a working stone within a sealed, cleansed protective circle. Once carefully removed from its protective wrapping, the shaft end of the feather is cut on a diagonal near where it was adjoined to the bird's wing, exposing its central hollow core while enabling the cut end to make comfortable yet firm contact with the heel of the adept's hand as he casts his intention. The removed piece of feather shaft is retained to be returned to nature in the same way as with botanical offcuts. The feathery strands of the feather are "dressed" by gently brushing and arranging the feather's strands so that they sit in perfect symmetry before returning the feather to its protective wrapping until it is to be used.

Feather wands crafted and used in this way are particularly suited to casting intentions over long distances rather than ones directed to recipients that are in close proximity. Consequently, they are normally used immediately after they are crafted from within the same protective circle, as there is no need for the recipient to be present or for the adept to travel to the recipient's location in order to cast the intention effectively.

The most potent feather wands are crafted from feathers garnered from the following birds: the crow, for energy and tenacity; the eagle, for strength and power; the dove, for love, affection, and gentility;

the raven, for curses and counter-curses; or the hawk, for intensity and focus.

While not a common magical device, the feather wand serves a unique purpose, eliminating the need for the much more complex and time-consuming workings required to cast intentions over long distances.

Bones as Wands

What at first may seem a particularly barbaric and cruel practice, crafting wands from freshly slaughtered animal bones is an ancient Druidic practice that is much less unsettling when considered in the context of its origins.

At the peak of the pagan culture that gave rise to the learned Druids who devised the lore we adhere to today, the ancient population of the British Isles and Ireland was settled in small groups that consisted of extended families and people whom they had grown close to during their nomadic lives as hunter-gatherer tribes. These settled groups slowly expanded and were added to by others with similar needs, forming the clans that made up the well-documented pre-Celtic villages. One of the most beneficial aspects of these newly expanded settled groups was that, since there was no longer a need for the time-consuming functions of the hunter-gatherer, many of the individuals within the clan became "specialists" in a particular aspect of clan life. Some became farmers, planting, harvesting, and storing crops for the winter season; others raised animals, breeding them to increase the herds and keeping them in enclosures to establish the first domesticated herds. Many others developed skills for particular crafts, such as weaving, pottery, and carpentry, while yet others became the builders of the family huts, walls, and defenses that were so essential to the clan's safety and well-being. Only a few individuals became inspired to observe their surroundings and search for an understanding of the cycles of nature, the chaotic events of the weather, the cycles of day and night, the waxing and waning of the moon, and the nature of the tides. These were the original learned intellectuals, the ancient pre-Celtic Druids, who used their observations and deductions to help their communities prosper. In addition to these physical concepts, the Druids understood that there was an invisible, supranatural energy or force that both defines and powers all of these physical events, and that this spiritual energy was an integral and inseparable part of nature and all that exists within it.

The numerous animals that were bred and lived within the clan's village were nurtured either as protectors or warning givers, such as dogs and geese, or as a source of food, as in the case of cows, pigs, sheep, deer, and various fowl. The essential skills of the herdsmen who raised and tended the cattle, pigs, and sheep needed to feed the clan included the effective slaughtering and butchering of the animals. The meat the herdsmen produced was then bartered among the other members of the clan so that the essential necessities of each individual's life were distributed among the whole community. It is reasonable to assume that no part of the slaughtered animal was wasted and by far the majority of each animal was consumed as food. Any small portion that was seen as inedible was most likely fed to the guard dogs that protected the village every night. Given the high value of all the parts of any slaughtered animal, it reflects the importance that the members of the clan assigned to the Druids' workings and rituals that they offered some of the bones of freshly killed animals to be used as magical devices rather than keeping them all for cooking. Though the practice of crafting wands from the bones of newly killed animals may seem distasteful to modern-day sensitivities, it is a lasting aspect of inherited Druidic lore. *Bones used as living wands* play a unique part in Druidic culture. It is important to emphasize that all the animal bones used for wands by our ancestors and in today's practices are by-products of the essential food supply and that no animals in ancient times were or are now killed specifically or solely in order to use their bones as magical devices.

The bones used to craft living bone wands are derived from a number of different animals. Most often they are the leg bones or rib bones of cows, sheep, or deer. Once again, as with the other living wands we have seen previously, the provenance of the animal is of immense importance. The most sought after and suitable animal is one that is hunted in the wild. If using bones from a captive animal, its welfare, diet, and living environment must be taken into account. Each of these elements will affect the animal bones in the same way as they do the botanicals. The adept should never use any bones from commercially reared or industrially slaughtered animals, or bones purchased from stores, markets, or butchers.

Living bone wands should be crafted within a sealed, cleansed protective circle. When using these living wands, the adept's projected intention is channeled through the vital, living core of the bone, which means that it is channeled through the bone marrow in its core cavity. As each bone is a living part of the animal, a bone used as a wand is kept intact and not cut or shaped. However, when using small fowl bones as wands they are normally sharpened to a point at their tip. For all other bones, the crafting consists of simply cutting away any extraneous sinew and flesh and cleaning the surface of the bone with fresh spring water. As usual, the bone wand is secured in its protective wrapping until it is to be used. As with other living wands, bone wands should be used as soon as possible after crafting. While botanicals hold their essential energies in the wood's sap, with bones these energies are contained within the marrow (though this does not dissipate as quickly as tree sap).

Living bone wands are most often used in circumstances where animals themselves are the recipients of the adept's intention, such as for fertility intentions, longevity intentions, welfare intentions, and protection intentions. Historically they have been used to cast counter-intentions to dispel unwanted malevolent energies that may have been bound to animals.

There are also many recorded instances of living bone wands, in the form of protective wands, being used as apotropaic devices deposited in homes, farm buildings, gateways, and even manor houses and castles. Recall our discussion of protective wands and devices earlier in this chapter. In some instances, animal bones being used as protective deposits have been discovered in chimney breasts, buried beneath hearths, or hidden around doorways, windows, and hatches, having been placed there to prevent unwanted energies from entering. In other cases, entire horse skulls have been unearthed beneath gateways, and in a number of other incidents large collections of horse skulls have been found deposited under flooring boards in houses and inns as a means of protecting those on the upper floors from malevolent energies suspected to inhabit the downstairs levels. The majority of these apotropaic deposits have been dated to the late medieval period; as such they are quite possibly related to witchcraft, but to date no detailed understanding of the deposition ritual or the specific beliefs associated with it has been determined.

MALEVOLENT LIVING WANDS

As well as being a potent and versatile magical device, the living wand can also become a dangerous and powerful weapon if it falls into the hands of a malevolent practitioner. When used in the proper way, a living wand is a beneficial and curative device, but when used as part of a malicious working it can bring hurt and disaster upon the individual, object, or place to which its power is directed. While most of the living wands we have already discussed are imbued with beneficial attributes, there are a good number of tree species and other botanicals whose attributes and characteristics may be used for both good or bad intentions, and indeed there are a small number whose attributes may hold no beneficial virtues at all and, as such, living wands crafted from these species are employed only for harm and malicious intent. Although there will be no detailed instruction on the use of these *malevolent living wands,* it is important that the adept is familiar with them so that he may recognize them and the results they produce in the event that he encounters them in his work. With this familiarity, the adept has the ability to protect himself and others from the influence of these wands. We shall also see as we progress that living wands that have not been returned to nature in the proper way after they have been used may subsequently be adapted for improper workings and used to undo all of the benefits they may have been crafted to deliver.

Inherent Risks

Before embarking on this topic, it is important to understand the inherent dangers in working with any form of living wand. The unique methods of working with living wands expose the adept to considerably more risk than using any other forms of magical devices. When using a living wand, the adept connects his internal energies directly with the living vital sap at the core of the wand and therefore with the fundamental, elemental forces in the wand, exposing himself to their direct influence; this process, in many if not most cases, may affect every area of the adept's physical and spiritual existence. Should the adept or any external third party reverse the intended direction of the flow of the casting, the results could be catastrophic and permanent—this may be done accidentally as well as intentionally, and the risk of doing harm is extremely high.

According to the ancient lore of the Druids, within nature there are a great deal more potentially malevolent botanicals than there are malign tree species. Fortunately, however, both are hugely outnumbered by the overwhelming number of beneficial trees and plants that make up our meadows and forests. Many adepts would argue that there are, in fact, no trees or botanicals that have *solely* malevolent characteristics. According to this logic, since trees and botanicals are principally imbued with attributes that amplify and empower the personal energies of the adept, if the adept channels his malevolent intentions through the core of a wand they will inevitably be magnified in the same way as benevolent intentions, giving rise to malevolent wands. So it may follow that no trees or other botanicals are invested with intrinsically malevolent attributes, but rather that the enhancing attributes they have may be utilized in a malign way. It is this *misuse* of the wands' attributes that we shall be examining here.

Most living wands used to cast curses and malicious intentions, in other words most malevolent living wands, are crafted from either oak or rowan wood. Oak wood is favored because of its association with strength and its ability to amplify the intention of the adept. Rowan wood is also favored because of its strong connection with the spiritual realm and its historic use in witchcraft and curse casting. Living wands crafted from either of these species may have their malign attributes compounded by wrapping them with entwining botanicals such as ivy, mistletoe, hemlock, briar, or nettle. Both oak and rowan wood may also be combined with wood from nightshade, holly, or gorse plants in order to craft a compound wand with significant malevolent power.

Typically, malevolent wands are crafted as simple, rudimentary wands. Having said that, they may also be crafted further, in any of the various forms we have seen previously. The wood from whichever species have been chosen is crafted in exactly the same way for malevolent wands as in the case of benevolent wands. There is a difference in that often wands used to cast curses are much shorter than other wands. It has been suggested that this may be because these wands are often used in secretive ways, without the knowledge of the recipient of the curse, so they may have shorter shafts so that they can be more easily hidden. If we consider the simple rudimentary wand being crafted to cast a malign intention or curse of any kind, the donor tree would be identified using the exact same criteria we have already seen, the external influences on the tree would be considered in the same way, and all of the other steps for harvesting would be followed in the same way as well. Once harvested, the branch would be secured in its protective wrapping in the usual way until it is to be crafted.

The crafting of a malevolent wand takes place within a sealed, cleansed protective circle in order to both protect the wand from the influence of unwanted spiritual energies and to contain the malign nature of the wand and the working from the outside world until it is cast directly toward the recipient. The wand branch is cleansed in the usual way as it is equally important to avoid unwanted contamination and retain the integrity of a maleficent wand as it is with any other wand. Some would suggest that it is even more important to ensure the integrity of a malevolent wand, as any deterioration or inaccuracy affecting its use may produce even more harmful and damaging results than with a benevolent wand. The physical crafting is done in the same way as we have seen, except that the accompanying intentions spoken by the adept during the crafting will be entirely focused on the amplification of the wand's malign attributes, as these are the attributes that will take precedence during the casting later.

It is important that a malevolent wand is used as soon as it is crafted, by casting the curse or malign intention immediately and while the wand is still secured within the protective circle. This is done not only to ensure that the wand retains its potency, but also to ensure that any malign influences it may have already absorbed will not escape into the mundane world outside. To cast the curse, the adept stands with his shoulders in line with the recipient so that when his arm is raised he may point the wand directly toward the person, object, or place that is to receive the curse. The composed intention for the curse is then silently repeated until it is firmly placed within the adept's mind. Following this, the adept gathers his internal energies from the three locations within his body where they dwell (the mind, the heart, and the solar plexus) and focuses them at the heel of his palm, where there is contact between his palm and the wand's core. This planted energy is then visualized as a sphere of pure, bright energy that is then amplified through the concentrated meditation of the adept until it can be no longer contained. At this point, the adept visualizes the spoken curse being wrapped around and absorbed by the energy sphere, raises the arm holding the wand, and points the wand toward the recipient. The curse is then cast as the adept speaks the composed curse out loud while visualizing the energy sphere and curse leaving his palm, being channeled through the core of the wand, leaving the wand's tip, and journeying to the recipient. When the curse arrives, it is visualized as being absorbed by the recipient and bound to the recipient permanently. Once the adept is convinced the curse has been absorbed and bound, he lifts his arm and points the wand toward the sky, where it is held as the adept returns his concentration to the mundane world. The casting is then complete, and the adept may relax. Now the decision has to be made whether to retain the wand and store it securely in the knowledge that it may subsequently be needed to lift or amend the original curse, or if it is to be destroyed and its material returned to nature. If retaining a malevolent wand, it must be secured carefully; if it is acquired by a third party, it may be used to lift the curse, undoing its harm, or to redirect the curse to the adept who originally cast it, binding it to him in perpetuity.

A final but very important point to remember is that living wands are created for the benefit of those who use them and of those who receive the benevolent intentions they cast. As is often the case, devices crafted for good can be appropriated by others with malicious intent. Using living wands in this unintended way involves considerable risk, as does using any magical device for purposes for which they are not envisioned.

SUMMARY

In conclusion, we have seen that the Druidic tradition employs a wide variety of living wands, which are crafted and used for very specific needs. Each living wand is ritually harvested from carefully chosen species of trees and sometimes botanicals. In a few relatively obscure situations, feathers or bones from birds or animals are harvested to craft living wands. The wand material is chosen for its intrinsic attributes and virtues in order to enhance whatever intention is channeled through it. The wand is crafted in a way that makes it possible for the adept to project his intention through its core.

All living wands have a number of aspects in common that may be listed as follows:

- The individual donor tree, bird, or animal from which the wand material is harvested is chosen by taking into account a number of criteria that affect its internal attributes as tempered by the external influences of its growing environment.
- Every living wand, no matter what its intended use, must be used while it still retains the vital living sap or core that contains it spiritual energy. This vital core begins to deteriorate as soon as the harvested branch, feather, or bone is removed from its donor

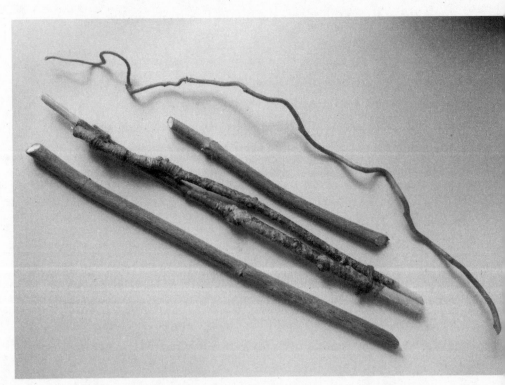

A group of living wands, each crafted for a specific use.

source, so the living wand must be used as soon as possible following its harvesting and crafting.

- Finally, it is imperative that each living wand is selected, harvested, and crafted for a specific need and that it is used only once.

The combination of these essential criteria make each Druidic living wand unique and imbues each wand with an unparalleled potency that can only be achieved through the powerful bonds among the donor source (the tree, other botanical, bird, or animal), the harvested material (the branch, feather, or animal bone), and the adept who plans to use the wand.

FIVE

Apposite Spaces

Finding and Preparing Your Workspace

As a living wand or other magical device approaches the point of its final use, its natural defenses are replaced by the specific attributes the adept has chosen to use and the wand becomes more and more vulnerable to unwanted external influences. The second stage of preparing a crafted wand for use, potentializing (which we will discuss in more detail in the next chapter), and the eventual casting are exceptional workings, which may attract unwanted and undesirable energies, either those that abide latently in the ambient atmosphere or those cast covertly by opposing adepts. Because of this, and as determined through millennia of experience, these final workings are always conducted in a very special space, a location where all undesired external influences may be neutralized while, conversely, the attributes and virtues that the adept has chosen to enhance her casting may be employed to best effect. Ideally crafting and cleansing workings should also take place within this space. Such apposite (meaning highly appropriate) spaces may not easily be found, especially in intensely urbanized environments. If the adept's casting efforts are to be employed to best effect, we must look both at how these spaces may be identified in the natural environment and, alternatively, at how such spaces may be emulated when the natural option is not available.

AUSPICIOUS OUTDOOR LOCATIONS

We have already discovered that our ancient Druidic ancestors were able to identify auspicious locations, as well as how these special places were chosen, to build their megalithic stone circles, standing stones, and burial chambers. We also know that ancient Druids and the nomadic pagan clans they served prioritized these important places, preferring to settle there than in more convenient locations closer to water supplies and arable land. This demonstrates how vital these auspicious places were to Druidic culture and spiritual welfare, and how community members were prepared to carry their water and other supplies from distant sources just so they could live close to these sites and the spiritual energies they emanate. We have also explored one of the magical devices the ancient Druids used to locate such places, using their forked wands to detect the invisible energies that make these places so important. Today, we still use similar living forked wands to detect or *dowse* energy sources of all types, and these divining wands may indeed be employed to detect the same invisible energies that remain just as important as they were to our ancestors.

The simplest way to engage with these auspicious places, to see if they resonate with your own individual spiritual energies, is to visit an established site, to sit quietly with an open, receptive mind, and see if you are receptive to the particular energies of that site. If you feel your spirit is in harmony with that location and that it is readily available to you, then this is the place you should plan to undertake your important workings and ritual (such as potentializing and casting a newly crafted wand). If, for whatever reason, the location does not resonate with your personal energies, then search out another established site and try again. If this second site does not harmonize with you, then continue in your search until you find a responsive location. Experience has shown us that some sites resonate with some individuals but not others, while a small number of sites resonate with everyone that approaches them. This simple search may enable you to find an appropriate ritual space

The Seven Sisters stone circle near Killarney in County Kerry, Ireland.
(See also color plate 10.)

that has a proven history as an auspicious spiritual site for many thousands of years.

Unfortunately, these ancient sites only exist in what we could call the ancient Druidic homelands, and even then many are inaccessible to the general public as they are located on private land. The most practical solution to this dilemma is to search for a previously unknown sacred space using a living forked wand, or to simply follow your own intuition in the same way the ancient Druids did. Apposite spaces are most often found in natural, unspoiled rural places where the adept can find a quiet, peaceful, secluded atmosphere conducive to the workings and rituals in which they intend to participate. If you choose to employ your intuition you will find that subtle indicators will indicate potential sites; when such indicators are heeded, you will discover powerful energies that will leave you certain that the space you have discovered will become your ideal, lifelong auspicious location that you will return to time and time again.

If the adept lives in an intensely urbanized environment, there will not be many opportunities to explore the sorts of locations where an individual's harmonic energies may reside. In such a case, alternative sites may be created to serve a similar purpose. To fully understand how this may be done, it is necessary to look more closely at what defines an auspicious place and how the adept may plan to engage with it.

THE SEVEN CONDITIONS

When our ancient ancestors discovered an auspicious place, by whatever means, they instinctively knew that their ability to work with the energies and forces of nature was massively increased when they worked within it. The two most well-known examples of such locations are the Druidic grove, usually found deep within the ancient oak forests, or the stone circles that litter the landscape of the Druidic homelands. On rare occasions we see the combination of both of these locations when we discover stone circles erected within the confines of woodland groves.

Within the Welsh Druidic tradition that I grew up with, the discovering and developing of these auspicious places is determined by seven conditions referred to as the "Seven Stones," or *Saith Maen* in the native language. In this context the word *stones* is not to be taken in its literal sense, but as a metaphor for the seven *firm* or *solid* eternal rules that underpin Druidic workings. This relates to the alchemical vernacular of the famous *philosopher's stone,* which does not refer to an actual stone but to a secret body of knowledge that is solid and eternal in the same way as a stone may be perceived. The Saith Maen are one of the most closely guarded secrets of Druidic lore and, as with all of the other fundamental mysteries of Druidic lore, they are maintained only within the oral tradition and are taught exclusively by the face-to-face, teacher-learner methodology that is so well recorded in the history of the European Druids.

Each of the Saith Maen relate to the range of physical skills and spiritual insights necessary to identify these special places, including how to decipher the range of information that may be interpreted at the site and how to engage with the spiritual energies that are present. The first stone of the Saith Maen explores the indicators that will suggest to the adept that she is approaching or is within an auspicious place. The second describes a series of spiritual workings that confirm the location is indeed an auspicious place and ascertain the potential energies that are present. The third, fourth, and fifth stones describe in great detail the crucial observations required to identify the geographic orientation of the site, including how this may be engaged with and what potential the site may yield. The sixth stone reveals the information required to resolve what needs to be undertaken to engage most effectively with the site, determining whether it may be best to use the site as a ritual gathering place, a spiritual workspace, or a place of meditation and, having resolved these aspects, whether the site meets the criteria required to develop it as a formal stone circle. The seventh stone, the longest and most complicated one, gives instruction on the three stages of the creation of a stone circle: 1) the preliminary preparatory observations to determine the number of stones to be erected and their orientation and positioning; 2) the way the circle is to be erected; and 3) the elevation of the circle to its higher potential—also considered the spiritual empowerment of the site, connecting the physical circle with the spiritual energies present at the site.

This entire philosophy and the Saith Maen that govern it works on the assumption that such sites of focused, powerful spiritual energy are to be found at specific locations dotted around the natural landscape. This assertion is based on the experience and observations of untold generations of learned Druids over the six thousand or so years since the first auspicious sites were identified and the earliest circles erected. What we now need to consider is which of the Saith Maen are relevant to establishing an auspicious space for all of the adept's intended workings, rituals, and celebrations that does not depend on the discovery of an existing place of spiritual focus but that may be crafted in a previously "inauspicious" place by attracting similar spiritual energies that the adept may engage with. In doing this, we may have to forgo using the site for the observation and understanding of universal phenomena and events as, potentially, the site may be the adept's garden, kitchen, or workshop, but this does not prevent the establishing of a site of focused spiritual energies at a chosen location that the adept may then engage with.

At this point I should explain that as a lifelong Druid I am restricted in exactly which elements of the oral tradition I may disclose. The much-debated theories relating to the secrecy of the Druids and their unrivaled ability to memorize vast tracts of detailed oral lore are to some extent true. The reasons for this are many and have their origins in the fact that ancient Druids had no established form of writing, so they were obliged to memorize their lore. More importantly, various elements of the lore were and are taught in a particular sequence, each following the other as a means of building a body of knowledge without risking the inevitable consequences of the learner trying to engage with the more complex practices without first understanding the principles that underpin them and that are necessary to conduct them safely and effectively. However, a broad explanation of the Saith Maen, for example, conveyed in everyday language will enable the adept to understand the sequential processes involved in establishing an apposite site for workings without compromising the integrity of the long-held secret lore.

Assuming the adept does not anticipate finding an existing site of spiritual energy within her kitchen or garden, the first two Saith Maen may be abandoned, as they relate to the discovery and confirmation of an existing spiritual site within a natural landscape. The third, fourth, and fifth stones, however, that describe the crucial observations required to identify the geographic orientation of the site, how the site may be engaged with, and what potential the site may yield are essential. The sixth stone, revealing the information required to resolve what needs to be undertaken to engage most effectively with the site, is also very relevant in this instance, as is the seventh stone that gives instruction on the three stages of creating an auspicious space and crafting a stone circle (or a representation of one). Bearing in mind that the original Saith Maen were developed to be used in the natural landscape, each stone needs to be amended and adapted so that it relates not to identifying an existing auspicious space in nature but to crafting an auspicious space in an otherwise "ordinary" location—in other words, developing a space that is established not to utilize existent localized spiritual energies but to attract these potent energies and focus them within the location.

The third stone describes the observations required to identify and record the orientation of the site in relation to the rising or setting of the sun and moon at the appropriate season. (For instance, the point of the setting sun at the summer solstice.) This is important in establishing any ritual site, particularly if it is to be used for workings or celebrations that correspond to specific lunar or solar events such as solstices or equinoxes. The observations required include determining the date, time, and compass point of the sunrise, sunset, moonrise, and moonset in the location on each of these days—spring equinox, summer solstice, autumn equinox, and winter solstice. With these important facts established, the adept may choose the most significant orientation for their intended site.

The fourth stone explains how this orientation is relevant to the adept's intended use of the space and how she plans to engage with the site. For example, if the adept is female, she may choose to align the site with the female corresponding moonrise or moonset, rather than those events related to the masculine sun. Alternatively, if the space is intended to be used mainly for sex magic, it would be best to align the site with the sunrise on the spring equinox, as this is the most potent alignment for sex magic or fertility rituals.

The fifth stone explores what potential the site may yield. This defines which elements of the potential site may invoke the outcomes the adept most desires. The information revealed by the fifth stone will inform the later stones, which define the layout and construction of the site. If the site is intended to inspire the workings of divination, for example, this will mean that it should be constructed to include space for both the adept and the subject within its working area.

The sixth stone reveals the information required to assist the adept in defining the practical elements of the site's composition and focuses on whether it is intended to be used as a ritual gathering place, a spiritual workspace, a place of meditation, or any combination of these. Determining this will of course require some means of assessing the vitality of the spiritual energies associated with the site and whether these energies are potent enough for the intended use or whether they will need to be augmented or amplified by additional devices.

As indicated, the seventh stone provides instruction on the three stages of creation of a stone circle derived from millennia of observation, experimentation, and development. (The ritual site is still referred to as the *circle* even if it is a simple site in the adept's kitchen.)

Unfortunately, the detailed instructions contained within each of the stones cannot be revealed, but with the insights gained from all the workings explored previously and subsequently, in combination with engaging with her own intuition, the adept may compose her own rituals and workings to successfully achieve the intended outcomes of the Saith Maen and construct a very effective site.

CONSTRUCTING AN AUSPICIOUS WORKSPACE

In the absence of the ability to conveniently access an established sacred Druidic site, the space described in the following section will function perfectly well as an apposite site for any or all of the workings related to the use of Druidic living wands. In particular, it will provide the ideal space for the potentializing of the wand, the meditative composition of the adept's intention, and the final casting of the intention using whatever magical device the adept has chosen.

If the adept chooses to construct her own auspicious working space for the workings that follow, the most appropriate composition is based on the *Eternal Sigil,* a combination of the arcane Druidic symbols for the sun and the Earth that, when combined, represent the eternal relationship between the Earth and the sun, between nature and the giver of life.

The sun is represented by a simple circle: ◯

The Earth is represented by a horizontal cross: ┼

The two combined create the representation of eternity: ⊕

All of these Druidic sigils are seen repeatedly in many of the megalithic sites around the British Isles and Ireland—carved into standing stones, the Irish and Welsh ogham stones, ancient trees, and funereal wares. They are also used in many Druidic workings and rituals.

An Eternal Sigil etched into an ogham stone near the Gap of Dunloe, Killarney, Ireland.

In using the Eternal Sigil as a magical device, by drawing or carving it on the working stone (or work surface), it must first be aligned with the auspicious orientation chosen by the adept. This orientation is typically the compass point of the rising sun on the summer equinox and may be determined by either referring to local publications or by direct observation. The methodology we will explore in the following example may be applied when establishing an indoor or outdoor working space.

The area of the intended site needs to be sufficiently large to contain the working stone (which may be as simple as a wooden table), four small bowls that represent the four cardinal points of the space, and enough room for the adept to move around the space comfortably. The site must also be situated in a place that allows the adept to cast a protective circle around its periphery.

Establishing an apposite site begins by selecting a central point for the Eternal Sigil, ensuring there is enough room around it for all of the considerations just described. Standing at the center point, use a compass to determine the direction of the orientation (in relation to the chosen setting or rising of the sun or moon on the intended date of the working) and then place the first of the four bowls at the periphery where the chosen line intersects it.

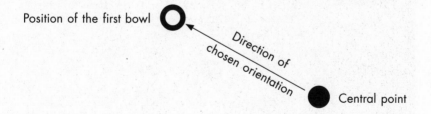

Position of the first bowl

Direction of chosen orientation

Central point

The line is then extended to the opposite side of the central point and the second bowl is placed at the intersection of the line with the periphery.

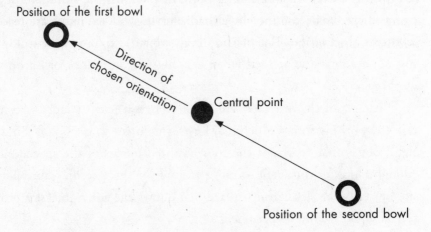

The final two points defining the space are positioned by measuring a line that is at a 90-degree angle to the first line and placing the two remaining bowls at the points where the line intersects with the periphery, as before.

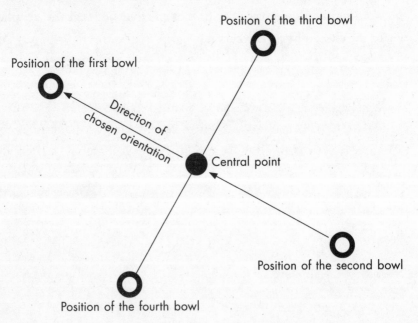

This process establishes the Earth sigil, a cross shape with its axis oriented to the chosen direction. The sun sigil, in the shape of a circle, is now superimposed upon it (in the same way as the Earth sigil was drawn or carved). The central point of the Earth sigil becomes the center of the circle, and the circle's radius is determined using the positioning of the four bowls at the cardinal points.

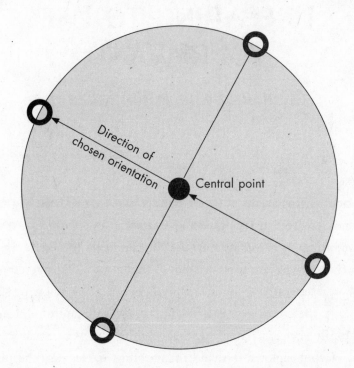

With this, the establishment of an auspicious space, in the shape of the Eternal Sigil, is complete. If left in place with permanent markings, this space may be used often for a wide range of workings and rituals.

SIX

PREPARING TO USE YOUR WAND

Cleansing and Potentializing

O nce a living wand, staff, or bundle has been successfully crafted and secured in its protective wrapping, every urgency must be employed to use it before its spiritual energies begin to deteriorate. This means that it *must* be used within six hours of being harvested and crafted or, if harvested at night, within six hours of the following sunrise. As a result, the creation of each living wand needs careful and meticulous planning, from its harvesting to its use through its eventual return to nature. Having explored in detail the selecting, harvesting, and physical crafting of a living wand, we will now turn our attention to the essential stages of its cleansing and potentializing—in other words, the preparation of the wand for casting the adept's intention. First we will explore the cleansing of the crafted wand, the most common means of ridding the crafted wand of any extraneous, unwanted external energies.

CLEANSING

In chapter two, "Wood Lore," we discussed how to cleanse a harvested branch or other botanical prior to wand crafting. Now we will discuss in more detail *how to cleanse a crafted wand prior to using it to cast an intention.* Each living wand cleansing is undertaken within a protective circle that has been established, sealed, and cleansed in the way we have seen above (see page 59). The living wand, staff, or bundle, having previously been crafted and secured in its protective wrapping, is placed on the working stone along with the other materials you will need: a flask of moon-cleansed water, a nonmetallic medium-sized bowl, a clean linen cloth, and a lit candle in a candle holder.

Moon-Cleansed Water

To craft moon-cleansed water, begin with unpolluted water from a source known to be uncontaminated and not conditioned with any chemicals typically added to tap water. Collect this water in a clean, clear glass vessel. Place the filled vessel under direct moonlight, ideally under a full moon, and leave it there overnight. *Before the sun rises,* cover the vessel with a lightproof cloth. The moon-cleansed water may be kept wrapped in its lightproof covering—known as a "shadow cloak"—indefinitely until it is to be used. If the water-filled vessel is exposed to daylight or any artificial light source, it becomes contaminated and must undergo the moon-cleansing process again.

The goal of this cleansing working is to nullify any extraneous energies that may have influenced the wand since its crafting. Even though the wand has been retained in a protective wrapping, the adept must ensure that when it is used for the planned casting it is free from any external energies that may distort or reduce its spiritual potential. This allows only the prescribed attributes and virtues of the wand to influence the adept's projected intention as it is channeled through the vital core of the living wand. The cleansing leaves the wand, staff, or bundle in a purified state, imbued with only the

Materials laid out for a living wand cleansing working.
(See also color plate 11.)

attributes the adept has selected for. This being the case, it is imperative that the cleansing is done *immediately* before the casting to ensure that the wand maintains its state of spiritual purity. The adept should follow the steps for this working whether she is preparing to use a traditional wood wand, a bone or feather wand, a wand bundle, or a staff.

The living wand cleansing working begins with removing the crafted wand from its protective wrapping and placing it at the front center of the working stone. The first stage of the cleansing is *the external or physical cleansing.* This is achieved by bathing the surface of the wand in moon-cleansed water, which results in both the physical cleansing of the wand surface, removing any unwanted deposits (molds, grime, or foreign bodies) while at the same time washing away any surface contamination from unwanted, external spiritual energies. This part of the cleansing begins with the bowl being brought to the front of the working stone and the wand (or bundle) being held at its base with its tip resting inside the bowl. To cleanse a staff, the bowl is placed on the floor immediately in front of the working stone and the staff is held at its base with its tip standing inside the bowl. The moon-cleansed water is then poured over the wand, bundle, or staff so that it runs along its length and into the bowl below. The item being cleansed is then slowly rotated so that the cleansing water comes into contact with its entire surface. While rotating, the adept speaks a *cleansing intention* similar to the following incantation, or one of her own composition (see more on the composition of incantations or intentions in chapter seven, "Using Your Wand."):

> I ask that this water, drawn directly from nature's
> stream, cleansed and purified by the immaculate light
> of the moon, washes away any and all malevolent
> energies from this wand, eliminating all but those
> virtues intended for good and the benefit of all,
> neutralizing all extraneous, unwanted forces, and

protecting this living and vital wand from any future
contamination until it is returned to its natural
source.

Once all of the moon-cleansed water has anointed the wand and all of the wand's surface area has been covered, the water is placed aside and the wand, staff, or bundle is carefully dried using the clean linen cloth. When a feather wand is being cleansed, it is delicately "dressed" as it is dried (as we have seen in chapter four, "Wand Types") to ensure that all of its feathery strands are in line and symmetrical. The water accrued in the bowl, along with any remaining supply of unused water in the flask, is then poured onto the ground so that it may be absorbed back into nature. While doing this, the adept speaks the following or a similar self-composed *returning intention:*

Giving thanks to nature, I return this borrowed gift to
you with the intention that, in good time, it may be
used for the good purposes of others that follow.

With this, the bowl and flask are placed to the side of the working stone.

The next stage of the cleansing is *the internal or spiritual cleansing.* This is achieved by bringing the lit candle in its holder to the front center of the working stone. The adept holds the wand or other device horizontally, with one hand at each end. Then the adept passes the shaft of the wand slowly through the flame of the candle, though not so slowly that it chars, scorches, or burns. As the burning flame cleanses the spiritual interior of the wand, the adept speaks the following or a similar self-composed *cleansing intention:*

May this purifying flame cleanse the vital energies at
the core of this wand, expelling all unseen malevolent
forces, leaving only those virtues and attributes
intended for good and the benefit of all. May it sear
and consume all unwanted influences and protect

against all future incursions until this wand is
returned to its natural source.

Once this flame-cleansing is complete the wand is once again wiped clean with the linen cloth, removing any accumulated soot from its surface.

This completes the external/physical and internal/spiritual cleansing of the wand or device following its crafting and before casting. The wand is now ready for the next stage of its preparation before the casting is undertaken: potentializing. From this point forward, the adept must be aware that there remains a risk that the cleansed wand or device may again be corrupted or nullified by external influences. Having been cleansed, the wand may have lost some of its natural spiritual defenses and may now be at its most vulnerable. With this in mind we can see that cleansing a crafted wand *must* be done at the last possible moment before the device is to be used. Once the cleansing has been completed the wand or device is again secured in its protective wrapping in preparation for potentializing.

POTENTIALIZING

The next and final stage of a wand's preparation for casting is its spiritual *potentializing,* wherein the attributes and virtues required to enhance the adept's casting that have already been imbued to the wand or other device are amplified to release their maximum potential and elevate their natural energies from the mundane to the metaphysical, from the everyday to the spiritual, and from the dormant to the dynamic. This elevation can only be achieved in very singular, exceptional places, where the boundaries between the mundane and the spiritual are at their thinnest, where the adept may cast her intentions across and through these barriers so that they may journey safely and arrive intact at their intended recipient, object, or location. We have just explored these apposite places in the previous chapter.

With the final crafting of the living wand complete and the apposite ritual site having been established, the adept can begin the working that elevates the living wand, staff, or other device to the zenith of its potential, promoting it to arguably the most potent magical device available to any Druid. This potentializing involves a profound ritual that must be undertaken within an auspicious space safeguarded by a protective circle cast around it. In this way the living wand is elevated, using the accumulated spiritual energies concentrated within the auspicious space, and protected from all unwanted malevolent external influences for the brief period between its elevation and its intended use for the planned casting.

Now we will discuss *how to potentialize a crafted wand prior to using it to cast an intention.*

Before the working can begin, a protective circle needs to be cast around the auspicious site. (To review the process for casting a protective circle, see page 59.) The adept will need a ceramic bowl containing enough pure sea salt to cast and, later, seal the circle, and two tall candle holders with lit candles. With these elements in place, the adept begins by undertaking their personal physical and spiritual cleansing to ensure the integrity of all that follows. As the orientation of the auspicious space and its working stone have been predetermined using the conditions we explored above, the entry portal has already been established on the side of the space opposite to the working stone and in direct alignment with the centerline of the established compass orientation. Standing outside of the defined space, the adept begins by placing one of the lit candles on each side of the entry portal, leaving a space of approximately three feet between them, allowing access to the inner space. Then, with their back to the working stone and beginning at the candle on their right, the adept begins casting the circle by spreading a thin line of sea salt, moving in a clockwise direction around the periphery of the site until arriving at the second lit candle at the entry portal. The adept then places the bowl with the remaining salt on the floor near the entrance. This enables the adept or other participants to enter or leave the circle before it is sealed and cleansed for the ritual.

The first stage of potentializing is to arrange the working stone within the protective circle. The living wand, still secured in its protective wrapping, is placed in the center of the working stone with a lit ritual candle held in a candle holder positioned at the rear of the stone, directly behind the wand. To the left of the wand place a nonmetallic goblet, and to the right place a flask of ritual metheglyn. If the adept is unable to access ritual metheglyn, a similar though not as potent substitute may be made by macerating a combination of equal quantities of freshly harvested (not store-bought) mint, meadowsweet, thyme, sage, and rosemary herbs in good white wine, cider, or, if possible, mead for at least forty-eight hours and straining it through a fine sieve. This herb wine may be stored and used as a substitute for metheglyn in workings when required. A medium-sized ceramic bowl and a clean linen cloth are also placed on the working stone for potentializing, together with a bunch of newly harvested oak leaves still on their stalks that have been assembled into a posy (or bouquet) and bound in a way that enables them to be used as a small brush, or *aspergillum,* to distribute the ritual metheglyn.

Once the materials are arranged, the adept enters the protective circle and then seals and cleanses it in the same way as we have seen before. The potentializing of the wand begins with the adept standing before the working stone. Bringing the goblet to the front of the stone, fill it with metheglyn. The adept then raises the goblet and speaks the following or a similar self-composed *libation intention:*

> *This libation, itself a gift of nature, is to be used to form an unbreakable bond between it and the potent energies of nature. It unites nature with my own spiritual being and the wand that is to channel and amplify my spiritual intention. Each to have its share and all to be empowered.*

With this, the adept takes a drink of the libation, then says:

*To me, my share. May it empower my spirit and
amplify my energies.*

Then the adept pours a little of the libation on to the ground,
saying:

To the Earth, your share, in gratitude for your gifts.

Bringing the bowl to the center of the stone, the tip of the wand is
placed inside the vessel and the libation is slowly poured over its shaft.
As it wets the wand, the adept speaks the following or a similar self-
composed *potentializing intention:*

*I anoint this wand with this sacred libation, uniting it
with a common bond to my spirit and the energies of
nature, elevating and empowering its inherent virtues
and creating a spiritual bond among all three.*

The wand is then placed onto the stone. The adept picks up the
partially filled bowl in one hand and the oak leaf posy in the other.
Dipping the posy into the metheglyn in the bowl, the adept gently
sprays the libation into the air while saying:

*I call upon the airborne energies of nature and our
ancestors to elevate this wand, amplify its vital
attributes, and channel my intentions to best effect.*

The adept then lifts the wand once again and passes the wet surface
of the wand through the lit candle flame while saying.

*Empowered by the vitality of water through the
libation, of air and earth by their distribution,
and of fire through this flame, I bond nature's
elemental energies and spirits, uniting them
through this sacred ritual so that they may be used*

for the benefit of those casting and receiving the forthcoming intention.

The wand is then wiped dry using the linen cloth and placed on the stone. The candle flame is extinguished, and the remaining libation is poured on the ground while the adept says:

What is lit is extinguished, what is given is returned.

The wand has now been elevated to its potential and *must* be used to cast the planned intention as soon as possible, before the energies of the potentialized wand begin to dissipate.

SMOKE INTENSIFICATION

Even after a wand has been used to cast its intention it still retains some part of its elevated energies. This is one of the reasons why *discharged wands,* living wands that have been used to cast their intentions, must be kept somewhere safe until they are destroyed and returned to nature. It is partly their retained energies that allow such wands to be used to amend or nullify the intentions they were initially used to cast. These retained energies may also be used to further elevate a second wand, raising it even higher than a normal potentializing working. This *smoke elevation working* is fairly complex in its preparation and, as with most of the other living wand workings, it is unique to the Druidic tradition.

The working is undertaken within a protective circle both to prevent unwanted external energies from influencing the wand and to ensure that the energies released by the working cannot escape the circle and influence any other ambient energies in the surrounding environment. The working stone is laid with a small brazier (a pan for holding burning coals) in which to burn the wand, a small amount of kindling and a match, a vessel of moon-cleansed water, a ceramic bowl, and the discharged wand along with the newly crafted wand

Materials laid out for a smoke elevation working.

that is to be elevated—both in their individual protective wrapping.

The working begins with the adept removing the newly crafted wand from its wrapping and holding it in her left hand, placing the tip into the ceramic bowl. The water vessel is lifted and a little is poured onto the ground as the adept speaks:

To the Earth, your share, in gratitude for your gifts.

The moon-cleansed water from the vessel is then slowly poured over the shaft of the wand as the adept rotates the wand to ensure that the entire surface is wetted by the water. As this is being done, the adept speaks the following or a similar self-composed *potentializing intention:*

> *I anoint this wand with this purified water, uniting it with a common bond to my spirit and the energies of nature, elevating and empowering its inherent virtues and creating a spiritual bond among all three.*

With the anointing complete, the wand is held high with both hands as the adept says:

> *I call upon the sublime forces of nature to enter this gift and elevate its energies beyond the normal so that it may invest any intention that is channeled through it with all that is good and desirable.*

With the initial potentializing complete, the wand is placed aside on the working stone to await the second step—the smoke elevation.

The brazier is brought to the front of the stone. The kindling is placed within it and ignited to form a small fire. The discharged wand is then removed from its wrapping and broken into four pieces while the adept says:

> *Having served its desired purpose, I now break this wand, binding its work forever and preventing any future misuse.*

The four parts of the broken wand are then placed into the brazier with its small fire as the adept speaks the following or a similar self-composed *smoke elevation intention:*

> *I release the essential energies of this wand and transfer their spirit to the ensuing smoke to be absorbed by the new wand, adding to its potency,*

increasing its power, and elevating it to the highest level.

As the discharged wand's remains begin to smoke, the adept lifts the new wand and, holding it with a hand at each end, positions the center of the wand's shaft in the rising smoke while saying:

I bring this wand to the smoke and hold it within. May it absorb the latent energies released by its predecessor and add them to its already considerable power. I ask this in the name of all those who have gone before and those who will follow.

The wand is held in the smoke until it subsides. The adept then secures the wand in its protective wrapping until it is to be used. The burned ashes of the original wand are placed in a container until they can be returned to nature.

SEVEN

USING YOUR WAND

Casting and Reworking Intentions with
Basic Wands, Staffs, and More

The fundamental purpose in crafting all wands is to use them as a means of channeling the adept's intention and projecting it toward its recipient. The reason the wand undergoes such scrupulous crafting is so that when the intention passes through its vital core it absorbs the beneficial attributes inherent in the original wood that have been so meticulously nurtured and amplified by the adept's magic workings. Even though the wand plays this essential part in the casting, the fundamental element of every casting is the intention. The intention itself is the ancient Druidic form of what other belief systems may call a spell, incantation, prayer, or even, in some cases, a curse or counter-curse. It is the way a Druidic adept, or Druid, intentionally casts a specific invisible force, spirit, or energy to be bound to its recipient. The intention may be a desire to empower an individual, bind an individual in love, stimulate an attraction, or cleanse a person, object, or space, and so on. The recipient may be a person or persons, an object, an animal or animals, a place, a home, and so forth; it may be either animate or inanimate.

Druids within Nature

Druidic lore tells us that we are all an equal part within nature. The word *within* is most important in this context. Unlike many other belief systems, Druidic lore explains that all living things are equal and interdependent; no one and nothing can reach their full potential without the recognition, respect, and integration of all of the other physical and spiritual elements within nature as a whole. We have seen that all living entities are imbued with three cardinal essences, and that all living things share at least one of these spiritual essences: the communal energy, or world spirit. As we all share this universal energy, it is possible for each of us to communicate our thoughts, beliefs, and intentions to every other living thing in our universe. This includes those living things that some believe we cannot communicate with because, at face value, they lack the physical attributes we humans use to speak, listen, and see.

In simple terms, the fact that we share this communal energy means that we are able to communicate with all living things, with individual entities or with the whole of nature at once. With this in mind, we can see that when we wish to communicate intentions during rituals or other workings, or when we cast intentions using living wands, we communicate on a spiritual basis directly with the intended recipient.

Unlike prayers and incantations, the Druidic intention does not attempt to invoke a deity or request any god's intercession, because, as we have seen previously, there are no gods or deities in Druidic lore. Instead, the intention focuses and concentrates the potent energies of nature to enact the adept's purpose. Each intention is composed by the adept to address a specific need, in anticipation of a perceived difficulty or in response to an individual circumstance. Contrary to much speculation, there are no "standard intentions" in the massive corpus of the Druidic oral tradition; there is nothing that may be referred to as a guide and nothing that needs to be committed to memory. The adept must compose each and every intention in response to the specific need before him, just as we have seen with the crafting of each unique living wand. Having said that, there are a number of imperatives that guide the Druid in the *composition of intentions*—principles that over many millennia have proven to benefit both adept and recipient. These may be summarized as follows:

1. The purpose of the intention must be clearly and unambiguously stated in the simplest possible terms. The purpose of the intention is the basic reason the casting is to be undertaken.

2. The final result of the intention must be stated in the same clear terms.

3. The means and method of the intention must be clearly stated.

4. The recipient of the intention must be identified in such a way that they (or it) cannot be mistaken or misunderstood.

5. In order to avoid confusion, there should be no attempt to use arcane language in the composition. The intention should always be constructed in the native tongue of the adept who casts it.

6. The intention must include the binding element—wording within the composed intention that binds the intention to the recipient ("I bind the intention to *[Name]*")—and a statement of gratitude at its close.

7. The intention may be composed beforehand in preparation for the casting and may be written or memorized for use during the casting.

8. Each intention must be unique, never reused but not discarded until the intention has been seen to work. Bear in mind that in some instances of curses and counter-curses, the original intention must be repeated for any form of annulling or lifting the intention.

9. When casting the intention, the adept may speak it out loud, whisper it quietly, or recite it mentally without spoken words. All methods have equal effect.

Although each intention must be carefully composed for each individual casting, here is an example of how the principles listed above may be used to compose a typical intention before it is cast. The example applies the imperatives in the same order as they appear above.

> *I cast this intention in order to bring two people together and bind them in love and affection. May they live from this point forth in harmony and in an unbreakable bond of mutual love for the rest of their natural lives. I do this by calling upon all the spiritual energies of the natural world to aid and empower me in my work and amplify the virtues of the magic I employ. I cast this intention and bind it to* [Name], *in order that it may open his eyes to the love of* [Name], *forge his response in a positive way, and build his undying love for her in return. May it result in their life-long friendship and adoration, for as long as they shall live. I bind together* [Name] *and* [Name] *with this casting. May they live long and happy lives in each other's mutual love. I and they respect the ineffable laws of the natural world and remain grateful for nature's abundant gifts.*

With all the necessary preparation complete, the adept is now ready to cast the intention. The method of casting will need to be modified according to the particular magical device being used. As we have seen these may vary from the simple rudimentary wand to the more complex compound wands, from the staff to the flying staff, or from the feather wand to a wand crafted from an animal bone. In other cases, apotropaic bundles may be used to cast intentions, or they may be deposited as a means of protection. We now need to examine each means of casting and each device being used so that a comprehensive understanding may be arrived at for every circumstance.

CASTING AN INTENTION WITH A WAND

Even though we have explored a variety of different wooden wands and have seen that each has its own attributes and characteristics, the method of using basic wands, such as rudimentary, entwined, or compound wands, to cast an intention is the same in every case. Having potentialized the wand and composed the appropriate intention, there are then *three successive stages required for every casting*. The first stage is the gathering and intensification of the adept's energies that will be used to carry the intention, the second is the focusing of the intention itself and its attachment to the intensified energies, and the third is the projection of the intention from the adept to its recipient. The first and second stages are accomplished within the adept's body. The third and final stage requires the use of the wand as an extension of the adept's spiritual being. In order for the wand to function as the channeling device for the adept's intention there must be an ideal connection or interface between the adept's body and the wand. This is achieved by holding the wand in the correct position in the hand, with the diagonally cut heel-end of the wand forming a firm contact with the lower palm of the adept, as shown in the illustration on the following page.

Once this wand grip has been mastered the three stages of the casting may begin. The adept should stand inside the protective circle that was cast in the apposite space established for this casting. The objective of the first stage of the casting is to gather and intensify the personal energies of the adept. This is done by concentrating the energies at the heel of the adept's casting hand as the projecting force to carry the intention. The casting energy is held at the gathering point at the interface between the adept's hand and the core of the wand. To gather the energies, the adept stands in the place from where he means to cast the intention, then relaxes his body by first relaxing the shoulders, dropping them to a resting position, and easing any tension in the muscles of the neck and shoulders. Then the

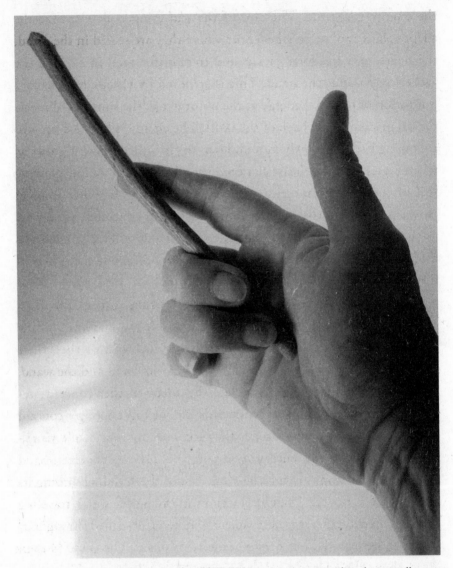

Hand holding a rudimentary wand for casting, showing the diagonally cut end of the wand, and consequently the wand's inner core, making direct contact with the adept's lower palm.

adept progressively continues to relax all the muscles starting from the neck and ending at the toes. Once fully relaxed, the adept then focuses on establishing a state of calm meditation before beginning the energy gathering. The aim of the gathering is to visualize the adept's sources of personal energies where they are seated in the mind, the heart, and the solar plexus and to transfer each in turn to the gathering point at the hand. This is achieved by visualizing the concentration of personal energy at the point where the spinal cord meets the brain stem at the back of the skull. The energy is bundled up into a glowing ball and slowly moved down to the heart where it grows as the energies from the heart center are combined with it. The glowing ball of energy is then transferred to the solar plexus where it again grows as it absorbs the energies from this seat. It continues its journey to the heel of the casting hand where the glowing ball of energy is held, or "parked," below the skin at the projection point at the heel of the palm.

To complete the second and third stages of the casting, the adept now points the wand toward the recipient and recites the words of the intention while visualizing the words being absorbed by the sphere of personal energies at the interface between the hand and the wand. When this visualization is complete the adept further concentrates the energy globe until his intuition tells him he can no longer contain it. At this point the adept recites the intention out loud while visualizing the concentrated energy traversing the interface between hand and wand, coursing through the vital core of the wand, absorbing its attributes as it travels. Then he envisions it leaving the wand, traveling to the recipient, entering the recipient and being absorbed throughout its entire being, whether person, object, or place. The wand is then lifted above the adept's head and pointed toward the sky. This completes the casting and the discharged wand is returned to its protective wrapping to await its return to nature as described in the next chapter. It is important to emphasize that neither the intention's wording nor the wand itself may be reused for any other working. This casting method may be used for all types of rudimentary wands, entwined wands, or compound wands.

CASTING AND IMPRINTING WITH
A STAFF OR ROD

Staffs and rods are interchangeable in the way that they are used. Each may be used in one of two ways: to cast an intention from its tip, or as a device for "imprinting" an intention at a particular spot by stamping it onto the ground.

To use a staff or rod to cast an intention, the same preparation is undertaken as with a wand. With the adept standing inside the protective circle, the implement is held at the middle of its shaft with a firm grip. Once the adept's personal energies have been gathered and held at the heel of the hand, the staff is lifted from the ground and its tip pointed toward the recipient. The intention is then bound to the energy and concentrated until it cannot be retained any longer. At this moment the intention is recited out loud as the adept visualizes the energy sphere crossing the interface between the hand and the staff, traveling along the core of the staff as it absorbs the staff's attributes, and then journeying to the recipient and being absorbed. Once the intention has been absorbed by the recipient the adept raises the staff and points the tip toward the sky. The casting is now complete. If the intention is to be cast over a wider space, the staff is moved in a sweeping motion across the entire space as the intention is recited and cast in order to encompass the entire site.

To use a staff or rod to imprint an intention, the adept must first be standing in the location where the intention is to be deposited (the entrance of a house, a gateway, a pathway, a grove, or suchlike). He once again holds the staff at the middle of its shaft, gathers his personal energy in the way we have seen above, and holds it at the interface between hand and staff. The intention is then bound to the energy sphere and the staff is lifted approximately one foot from the ground. The intention is then repeated out loud and once completed the staff is brought down hard onto the ground to "plant" the intention and held there until the adept is confident that the intention is planted. The staff is then raised and its tip pointed to the sky as a sign that the working is compete. Then it is carried in a horizontal position away from the site so that it does not touch the ground again.

USING APOTROPAIC BUNDLES

Apotropaic bundles are used as protective devices, either by projecting an intention through the core of the bundle or by depositing the bundle in a vulnerable space to prevent unwanted, malevolent energies from entering. If using an apotropaic bundle as a projecting device, it is used in exactly the same way as a rudimentary wand. If using as a protective deposit, the adept's intention is to be absorbed by the bundle and not projected through its core.

The *deposition working for depositing an apotropaic bundle* begins with the adept at the location where the bundle is to be deposited. The adept's personal energies are again gathered at the interface between the hand and the bundle held within it. The intention is recited mentally as it is visualized as being bound to the energy sphere. When the concentrated energy may no longer be contained, the adept recites the intention aloud as the energy sphere is visualized as entering the bundle and being absorbed into its core. Once the protective bundle has been imbued with the intention it is deposited in the chosen place. It may be necessary to place a number of apotropaic bundles in various vulnerable places around a home, such as at widow openings, doorways, chimneys, hearths, and so on to provide impenetrable protection. Similarly, when protecting fields of crops or herds of animals it may be necessary to repeat the deposition working at every gateway, entry point, and barn door to ensure a secure protective defense. If securing a pathway or forest grove, all possible vulnerable points of entry need to be protected with the deposition of numerous bundles at every location. Such apotropaic bundles may remain in place indefinitely, providing protection for as long as they remain undisturbed. Indeed, many such ancient deposits have been discovered that appear to have been deposited many centuries earlier. Replacing protective deposit bundles with new, living bundles every few weeks, however, invigorates the intention and also allows the intention to be updated to reflect any changes in circumstance.

USING A FLYING STAFF

The flying staff is a unique device used exclusively to apply and reapply a psychotropic ointment to the body, enabling the subject to experience a planned visualized journey of her or his choosing. The ointment can be applied to any part of the body other than the face. The active ingredients are absorbed most effectively via the areas of the body covered by mucous membrane, the membrane that covers the exposed areas of the cavities of the body, such as the vagina. When male adepts use flying ointment, they typically apply it to the inner area of the forearm and wrist, and then sit with their forearms close to a fire so that the heat both dissolves the ointment and aids its absorption through the skin. As the active ingredients begin to take effect, the adept enhances his experience through deep meditation and visualization of the spiritual journey he has planned.

The unique aspects of a flying staff include the fact that it is not used to cast an intention beyond the adept, though the associated intention is channeled through the staff's core even if it is projected toward the adept himself. Also, the staff is used as a carrier to apply the flying ointment that is at the center of the working. Once the ointment has been applied with the flying staff, the adept's intention is channeled through the core of the staff, absorbing the attributes inherent within the staff as it does so, until it is taken up by the ointment, empowering the ointment with the accumulated spiritual energies it has been infused with on its journey. These additional attributes and virtues elevate the active ingredients within the flying ointment, fine-tuning them to the needs of the journey's objectives. Having already examined the preparation of the flying staff in chapter four, we must look at the crafting of the flying ointment before we can explore the flying wand working in detail.

Plate 1. The essential equipment for the harvesting rite, including a compass to establish the orientation of the donor tree and the selected branch.

Plate 2. Rudimentary living wand.

Plate 3. Entwined living wand, bound with freshly harvested ivy.

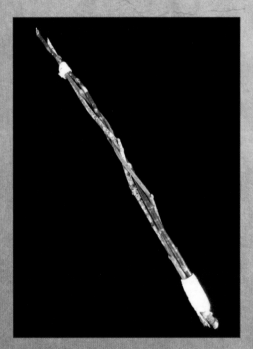

Plate 4. Compound living wand, with individual wands from three complementary tree species.

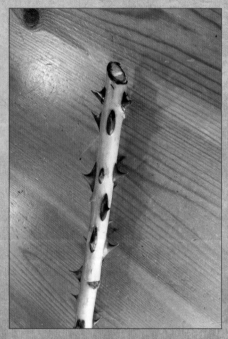

Plate 5. Rudimentary thorn living wand with its thorns intact.

Plate 6. The stone circle near the town of Kenmare in County Kerry, Ireland.

Plate 7. A typical collection of branches from protective tree species used to craft a living protective bundle.

Plate 8. A protective deposit bundle with a combination of complementary protective wood species.

Plate 9. A witch's broom, a possible version of the Druidic flying staff.

Plate 10. The Seven Sisters stone circle near Killarney in County Kerry, Ireland.

Plate 11. Materials laid out for a living wand cleansing working.

Plate 12. Newly harvested holly branch and rowan berries in preparation for the crafting of a living curse wand.

Plate 13. A collection of various cleansing herbs, including rosemary, mint, and lavender, to be used to craft a cleansing potion.

Plate 14. Materials laid out for the crafting of a cleansing potion.

Plate 15. Equipment for the return ritual, used to return a living wand to nature.

Caution!

Before beginning the crafting of any Druidic active preparation, like flying ointment, it is imperative to understand that all such crafting must only be undertaken by an experienced and learned practitioner. The description that follows *does not* contain sufficient instruction for anyone to safely attempt the crafting of flying ointment. Any attempt to follow these steps without additional instruction beyond this book may result in severe illness, lasting aftereffects, or even death. To craft any compound that includes poisonous botanicals requires many years of training and experience in order to correctly identify the botanicals used, understand the dire consequences of misidentifying deadly substances, and be confident in the exact strengths and quantities of the botanicals to be used. It is essential, therefore, that *no attempt is made to reproduce the crafting that follows.* For this reason, no quantities are given for any of the botanicals that are used.

Crafting flying ointment starts with harvesting the herbs used to craft the ointment while considering the same criteria as with all other harvestings, and the harvested herbs are secured in protective wrapping in the same way as branches for living wands. Once again, the crafting takes place at a working stone sealed within a protective circle. The working stone holds a lit ritual candle in a candle holder, a mortar and pestle, a small jug of moon-cleansed water, a small storage jar with a sealable lid to contain the crafted flying ointment, the harvested botanicals, a jar containing the rendered fat of a vixen or roe deer (mole or red squirrel fat are sometimes substituted), a wooden spatula to transfer the ointment from the mortar to its storage jar, and a clean linen cloth.

The botanicals used to craft flying ointment may include deadly nightshade, wormwood, poppy seed, yarrow, meadowsweet, rowan berries, and foxglove, each in precisely measured proportion.

Materials laid out for the crafting of flying ointment.

The working begins by pouring a little moon-cleansed water into the mortar, running it around the inside to ensure all of the surface is cleansed. The liquid is then poured onto the ground and the inside of the mortar wiped dry with the linen cloth. The same mortar is then turned over and its inner surface briefly passed above the candle flame to cleanse it with the fire. It is then wiped once again with the linen cloth before it is replaced on the working stone. The same steps are then repeated for the pestle. While all this is being done, the adept recites the following or a similar self-composed *cleansing intention:*

> *I cleanse this vessel with water and flame in*
> *preparation for the crafting that follows. May it be*
> *pure in its being and its spirit, free from any energies*
> *that may impair or distort its function.*

The leaves of each of the herbs are then removed from their stalks and placed in the mortar; the berries are removed from the stalks and they too are placed into the mortar, the contents of which are then ground until all are all combined and rendered to a fine paste. Sufficient roe deer fat is added to the paste and pounded to craft the resultant ointment. Any residual ointment on the pestle is removed using the spatula and returned to the mortar. The mortar is raised in both hands and held aloft as the adept recites the following (or similar) *elevation intention:*

> *Made from the gifts of nature to be used only for the*
> *benefit of all those involved, I ask that all the eternal*
> *energies of the cosmos combine to empower and*
> *elevate this complex and guide its use and influence*
> *upon those for whom it is intended.*

Returning the mortar to the working stone, the finished ointment is transferred from the mortar to the storage jar, which is sealed and stored until the ointment is to be used. This completes the crafting of the flying ointment.

Now we'll turn our attention to the flying staff working itself. The combined ritual for using a flying staff, requiring the application of the psychotropic flying ointment, deep meditation, spiritual visualization, and the projection of an intention through the staff's core, is a very skilled practice. It depends upon a high degree of focus, intense concentration, and mature intuition.

The subject of the flying staff working is most often the adept, whether male or female, or very occasionally a third party subject who would have to be well versed in the ways and workings of the Druidic tradition. The working typically takes place with the subject lying on the working stone within a protective circle, though the working stone may be substituted by a wooden table inside a similar protected working space. The ritual devices needed for the working are the flying staff, the flying ointment, a fire of significant enough size to generate heat to aid in the ointment's absorption, and a dark opaque cloth such as velvet used to cover the eyes and obscure all light. Before the working begins, the adept (or alternative subject) undergoes the cleansing of her body and personal energies. A range of cleansing methods can be used, including ritual bathing, moon cleansing, rain bathing, river immersion, and swimming. The following example involves a female adept as the subject of the working, using the traditional method, and should be adjusted to facilitate a secondary subject if required.

The adept first covers the first six inches of the tip of the flying staff with copious amounts of the flying ointment and places it beside the working stone in a position where it may be easily reached. The adept disrobes and lies naked on the working stone. Before picking up the loaded staff, the adept lies in a relaxed posture and initiates a calm meditative state. When ready, she visualizes the entire journey, from beginning to end, that she intends to take during the working. Once this has been completed, the adept takes hold of the flying staff near the upper end opposite the end smeared with flying ointment in such a way that she can use the staff to apply the flying ointment to the genital area. The first application of ointment is made by rubbing the loaded end of the staff on the inside of the vagina, the perineum, and the anal opening, ensuring that the ointment is transferred to the mucous membrane exposed at the vagina and the delicate skin on the perineum and anal entrance. (In the case of a male adept, the staff can be used to apply the flying ointment to the delicate skin of the penis, scrotum, perineum, and anal entrance—or to the inner arms, as instructed above.) The adept lies with her legs apart, exposing her vagina to the fire to aid in the skin's absorption of the ointment.

Once this is done, the adept lies back on the working stone or table and places the thick, lightproof cloth over her upper face to prevent any light entering the eyes. In the resulting darkness, with the staff held with both hands, the adept begins her focused meditation and embarks upon the first stages of the visual journey while waiting for the psychotropic agents to begin their work. As the transcendental journey continues, the adept begins to channel her desired intention through the core of the flying staff, casting the intention upon the recipient as the adept arrives at the intended journey's end. If, for example, the working is meant to cast an attraction intention, the adept's verbal intention may be:

> *I call upon the natural forces that govern us to instill within you* [Name] *a desire to seek out my presence, engage with me and be bound to me by a mutual attraction. May this desire remain with you until your life forces leave you and your body returns to nature.*

The adept enhances the experience and accelerates the effect of the ointment by reapplying ointment to the same bodily areas. As the spiritual journey continues the experience may become overwhelming and further applications may be impossible, and certainly not advisable. If this becomes the case, then the adept should submit herself to the journey and not reapply flying ointment as she will have absorbed sufficient active ingredients and further application may prove dangerous.

The working concludes when the adept completes her visualized journey and once again becomes aware of the mundane world. After completing the working, the staff is carefully cleaned in preparation for its return to nature.

The Druid's Staff and the Witch's Broom

Though the use of flying ointment and flying staffs by adepts, and specifically female adepts, is an accepted part of ancient Druidic lore, it is very possible that use of these traditions by the rural cunning folk of the time gave rise to the image of the medieval witch flying on her broom, and it may also account for why so many illustrations of the time show the witch naked astride her broomstick, with genitals in firm contact with the shaft of the broom. It is not difficult to imagine how the use of the adept's flying staff to travel on spiritual journeys may have been interpreted as a witch traveling on her broomstick. Indeed, there have been accounts of female adepts utilizing broom handles as impromptu substitutes for flying staffs, making the connection even more recognizable. It is impossible to definitively attribute the origins of the use of flying staffs to either Druids or witches, but it appears that at some point in history the tradition evolved into the flying staffs of Druidic lore and the more familiar witch's broom that corresponds with it in the witchcraft tradition.

CASTING WITH A FEATHER WAND

Feather wands are typically used in one of two ways, either to cast an intention over long distances, or to cast an intention over a sizable place or area. When using a feather wand to cast an intention to a recipient at a distance, or *over the horizon* as it is more often referred to, the method used is very similar to the use of a rudimentary wand.

The adept stands within an apposite space, secured inside a protective circle; the feather wand is held in a delicate grip with its hollow core in contact with the adept's hand. With the adept's arm raised horizontally, the tip of the feather is pointed in the direction of the recipient beyond the horizon. Then the same technique is used as when casting with a rudimentary wand, with the exception that the location of the recipient, whether a person, object, or place, is recited within the intention. When the casting is complete, the feather wand is pointed to the sky before being replaced in its protective wrapping until it is to be returned to nature.

When using a feather wand to cast an intention over a sizable space, such as a forest clearing, a house, a field, a herd of animals, or similar, the working is slightly more complex. The adept stands adjacent to the area over which the intention is to be cast. Typically this would not be near a working stone, so some form of table or bench is usually used to hold the necessary materials. Alternatively, the working tools may be laid on the ground or on any suitable and convenient flat surface. The materials needed include the feather wand, a bottle of moon-cleansed water, a medium-sized ceramic bowl, and a clean linen cloth. As is the norm, the adept will have composed the relevant intention beforehand.

The working begins with the adept holding the bowl in one hand and the open bottle of moon-cleansed water in the other. The bowl is held at waist height while the bottle is raised to shoulder height. The water is then slowly poured from the bottle so that it falls the two feet or so into the bowl below. As this is done the adept mentally recites the intention. The objective of this action is to both purify the water once again as it falls through the air and for the recited intention to be absorbed by the water as it falls. When the recitation is complete, the bottle is placed aside and any water around the rim of the bowl is wiped away with the linen cloth. Placing the cloth aside, the adept picks up the feather wand in the same grip as described previously. With the adept facing the left hand edge of the space he dips the tip of the feather wand into the charged water, lifts the wet feather into the air, and flicks the water from the feather tip toward the targeted space as the intention is spoken out loud. Slowly turning from the left to the right, the adept repeats this process until the entire space has been covered. Once this is done, the adept raises both the bowl and the feather wand high into the air and recites the following or a similar self-composed *empowerment intention:*

> **With the intention cast and bound, I call upon the eternal energies of nature to empower this working and prolong its presence for the benefit of all.**

The discharged feather wand is then returned to its protective wrapping until it is to be returned to nature.

Living feather wands are uncommon and are used only for the purposes just described. However, they are extremely potent and successful and therefore must be used with appropriate care and consideration. When the intention is directed to a person who may be a very long way away from the adept and as such completely unaware that the intention is being bound to him, careful consideration must be given to the consequences of the casting as the adept will not be present to witness the immediate results or the subsequent ramifications of his actions.

CASTING WITH A BONE WAND

While the living feather wand is crafted from a feather obtained from a chosen bird, the living bone wand is the only Druidic living wand crafted from an actual body part removed from the body of a deceased animal. As we have seen, such bones are taken from the animal carcass of an animal slaughtered as a food source—no animal is ever killed solely to provide bones for crafting wands. The choice of which bone to use depends on the animal species and the size of the animal. Typically, such bones would be various leg bones from a sheep, a pig, a boar, a roe deer, a goat, or other animals of a similar size that are slaughtered and butchered as part of the food supply. The chosen bone is cleaned, crafted, and potentialized as described previously, then secured in a protective wrapping.

Living bone wands are most frequently used in workings related to growth, crop productivity, cattle welfare, and other agricultural and cattle-rearing situations. The casting, therefore, is undertaken at the location of the need, where a temporary apposite space is constructed in the way we have seen before. The objective of casting with a living bone wand is to channel the adept's intention through the vital core of the wand, thereby imbuing the intention's energies with the unique attributes of the animal bone being used. In this instance, all that is needed for the casting is the wand itself. We shall use the casting of an intention over a herd of cattle to protect them from unwanted malevolent energies and assure their fertility as an example.

Arriving at the field, the adept positions himself at the location of the previously prepared apposite space, ensuring he has a panoramic view of the targeted herd of cattle. Facing the left extremity of the herd, the adept raises the wand to shoulder height with its tip facing the herd. The adept then moves the bone wand from its starting point across the entire herd to the right extremity while speaking the following *intention for casting with a bone wand,* or a similar self-composed recitation:

> *I channel this energy through the living bone of one*
> *of nature's fellow beings so that it may accrue the*
> *vital forces that live within and form an eternal bond,*
> *uniting all of nature's creatures as one world spirit. In*
> *doing this I ask that all of these vital, living energies*
> *may protect these beasts from all those malevolent*
> *forces that may wish to contaminate them and ensure*
> *their fertility and well-being throughout the years*
> *ahead.*

This simple casting completes the working, and the bone wand is then returned to its protective wrapping until it is to be returned to nature.

Living bone wands, although very effective and potent, are uncommon in today's practice for reasons that are not difficult to understand. They represent a means of connecting directly with nature in a way that may not be popular in many societies and may appear barbaric to many individuals in today's culture. They do, however, have their own place in Druidic lore as a magical device that has been utilized for millennia and one of the very few recorded in the early written accounts of those who may have lived in a time and place where Druidic culture was at its height.

CASTING WITH THE HAND

Casting an intention using the hand is obviously the most convenient and spontaneous means of projection, but what it gains in spontaneity it often sacrifices in subtlety. It may be argued that hand-cast intentions retain the full power and potency of the energies the adept has concentrated within his being while, alternatively, intentions may lack the amplification of the projected energies as passed through an external device like a living wand. It cannot be denied, however, that as an intention passes directly from the body when cast through the hand, it has no opportunity to be influenced by the additional complementary attributes and virtues of the carefully chosen woods and botanicals from which a living wand is crafted. In many instances, the adept chooses to cast an intention directly through his hand only when he is confident that all the attributes he desires may be accumulated from his own internal energies alone, and that in casting them he will effect the desired outcome without unnecessarily draining his own internal resources. There are, of course, circumstances when the adept may not have access to magical devices like living wands or staffs, and on such occasions the adept may have no alternative other than to use his hand. On other occasions, the adept may choose the unadulterated energy projected through the hand in preference to a more complex and time-consuming working using a device.

Hand casting may be undertaken from within an apposite space in order to protect the integrity of the projected intention, but most often it is accomplished spontaneously from whatever location the adept finds himself in at the time. In both instances the method of casting remains the same. The choice of which method to use is determined by the circumstances and the adept's intuition. As is usual in all castings, the intention—when time allows—is composed in advance. In cases where this is not possible the adept must be aware that all intentions cast spontaneously pose the risk of being less effective and less accurate, so even if time is short it always pays to give as much thought to the

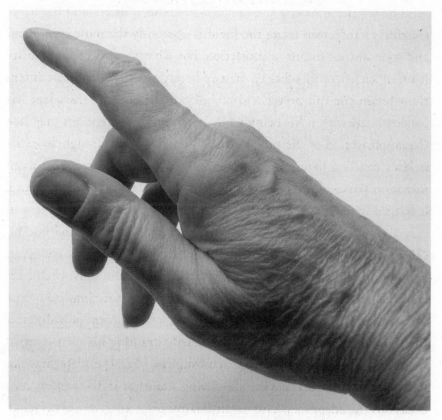

Hand positioned for hand casting of an intention.

wording of the intention as is possible before it is cast. The gathering of the internal energies and their concentration at the heel of the palm of one hand is essential, as when using devices, and cannot be eliminated. Fortunately, with experience and repeated practice, this may be achieved in very little time and, being aware that this may be a critical need, the adept should be prepared to practice and rehearse this gathering technique as often as is possible.

The working begins with the adept standing with his dominant side facing the recipient. When he senses the gathered intention cannot by retained any longer, the dominant arm is extended with the hand pointing toward the recipient. The intention is recited as it is visualized leaving the tips of the fingers, journeying to the recipient, and being absorbed and bound within them.

The intention having been recited, the arm is lifted, and the hand points skyward as the adept relaxes and returns focus to the mundane.

ANNULLING, UNDOING, AND REVERSING AN INTENTION USING THE ORIGINAL CASTING DEVICE

If the adept considers that there is even a remote possibility that the intention he has cast will need to be annulled, undone, or reversed then it is imperative to retain the original casting device so that it may be used in these workings. Only when the adept is confident that the intention has served its purpose should he consider returning the living wand to nature in the prescribed way.

It is important to distinguish the terms annulling, undoing, and reversing in the context of casting intentions, as the end result of each is very different. *Annulling an intention* means canceling the effect of the intention from the moment of the annulling without undoing the effects the intention may have had up to that point. *Undoing an intention* means canceling the effect of the intention from the moment of the undoing *and* undoing any effect that the intention may have had up to that point, thereby returning things to the original status quo that existed before the intention was cast. *Reversing an intention* means not only canceling the intention from the moment of the reversing but also invoking the exact opposite of the expected outcome of the original intention.

While the workings for all of these intentions have much in common, each is characterized by the different wording of the intention as it is cast. The fundamental thing they all have in common is that they all use the exact same device for the reworking (annulling, undoing, or reversing) as was used for the original casting, thereby retaining all the same properties and creating an immediate symbiosis that cannot be established through the use of a new device. The decision of whether to annul, undo, or reverse an intention is wholly dependent upon each individual circumstance and exactly how and why the original intention is to be revised.

If the original intention is simply not having any effect, then it is sufficient to annul the intention rather than leaving it to possibly cause an unwanted outcome at a later date. If the original intention has caused an unanticipated result, then it is best to undo the intention, returning things to their original state and then casting a second intention designed to achieve whatever it was that the first casting failed to do. If the cast intention has caused unanticipated problems or difficulties that not only need to be halted and undone (as is the case with an undoing) but also need to be corrected by further intentions to repair the damage, then the original intention needs to be reversed. In each reworking the living wand used to cast the original intention must be used.

In every Druid's workshop you will find a cache of wands that have been used for castings, labeled and stored in their protective wrappings just in case they may be needed to amend the intentions they originally cast. The decision to store the wands rather than return them to nature immediately following the casting, as is normally the case, will have been made by the adept either because he felt the cast intention was in some way flawed or vulnerable or because his intuition indicates that the wands may be needed again to amend the original workings.

If these wands are stored in this manner for any length of time it does of course raise the question of how they can still be classified as living wands when over time their vital sap evaporates and their essential energies dissipate. This degeneration would most definitely render any wand useless if an attempt were made to use the wand for a new working. But because of a wand's unbreakable association with its original casting the spiritual link is maintained, and the wand can therefore be used effectively in any working relating to its initial harvesting, crafting, and casting.

Whether the reworking is one of annulling, undoing, or reversing, the objective is still the same: to amend the original intention in some form or another. To do this effectively, the adept must emulate the original casting as closely as possible, working the new casting in exactly the same location with the same conditions as were present for the initial working. Again, the working for all three is essentially the same, the only variant being the phrasing of the intention. We know from what we have already seen that the wording of every intention is unique and must be composed by the adept who casts it, so the wordings that follow are meant only as guidelines to inspire the adept's own composition.

A typical intention for an *annulment working* may be phrased:

> *Though cast with good intent and bound to* [Name]
> *for their benefit and advancement, it is the case*
> *that my intention has not worked in the way it was*
> *envisioned. Therefore, with no ill purpose, I unbind*
> *the intention and release* [Name] *from its influence*
> *in all its forms and aspects. I further annul the*
> *intention and return its spiritual energies to nature*
> *with gratitude and due reverence.*

Once the annulment casting is complete, the wand is broken in two at its center point and placed aside in a secure location until it may be returned to nature.

A typical intention for an *undoing working* may be phrased:

> *Though cast with good intent and bound to [Name]*
> *for their benefit and advancement, it is the case*
> *that my intention has not worked in the way it was*
> *envisioned. Therefore, with no ill purpose, I unbind the*
> *intention and release [Name] from its influence in all*
> *its forms and aspects. I further annul the intention,*
> *and in addition I remove any effect that it may have*
> *caused and return all things to the place they were*
> *before my intention was cast. Now I return its spiritual*
> *energies to nature with gratitude and due reverence.*

Once the undoing casting is complete, as before, the wand is broken in two at its center point and placed aside in a secure location until it may be returned to nature.

A typical intention for a *reversal working* may be phrased:

> *Though cast with good intent and bound to [Name] for*
> *their benefit and advancement, it is the case that my*
> *intention has not worked in the way it was envisioned.*
> *Therefore, with no ill purpose, I unbind the intention and*
> *release [Name] from its influence in all its forms and*
> *aspects. I further annul the intention, and in addition I*
> *cast this renewed intention to counteract, reverse, and*
> *repair any unwanted circumstances that may have resulted*
> *from the initial casting. I return its spiritual energies to*
> *nature with gratitude and due reverence.*

Once the reversal casting is complete, the wand, once again, is broken in two at its center point and placed aside in a secure location until it may be returned to nature.

CASTING A COUNTER-CURSE

In addition to casting benevolent intentions, any of the magical devices explored above may also be used to cast malevolent ones with the purpose of bringing ill will, sickness, or even death upon the recipient. Such malevolent intentions, or *curses,* are rarely used and are most often employed by workers of the darker arts of Druidic lore, of which the associated history lists many. We will, however, assume that the curses we address here are cast by others and not by the adept himself, although the same counter-curses may be used in either instance. Before we explore the ways in which counter-curses may be cast and bound we must first fully understand the principles and methods of casting malevolent intentions or *curse casting* as it is more commonly known.

Danger!

Without doubt, the casting of malevolent intentions and the counter-castings that are used to counteract them make up the single most dangerous area of Druidic practice and, as such, great care must be given not only to its practice but also to its teaching as, once again, these potent rituals are part of the body of restricted Druidic workings we have encountered previously. We must remember here that along with the ability to cast malevolent intentions and the counter curses that are used to nullify them comes the responsibility for the consequences of both.

Principles of Curse Casting

Curses are cast in the same way as all other intentions, though typically there is much more secrecy associated with the casting itself. One of the reasons for this secrecy is that the technique used in counter-cursing can return the intention to the individual who originally cast it and bind it to him. Another and more feared outcome is that if the original device (wand) used to cast the curse can be found, it can be used not only to remove the curse from the recipient but also to bind it *irrevocably* to the individual who cast it, no matter what attempts he may make to remove it.

Many people associate the idea of casting curses with witches, sorcerers, and conjurers, but few connect curse casting with Druidic lore, forgetting maybe that all these cultures originate from the same folk magic tradition that gave rise to the cunning folk of rural prehistoric communities. It is true, however, that as each tradition developed and evolved many of their practices diverged, each giving priority to different aspects of what was originally the same tradition. While witchcraft became renowned for its darker practices before reemerging in a more benevolent light, the lore of the Druids became more involved with other elements of folk magic; the more malevolent side of Druidic lore became less prevalent, though it has never completely disappeared.

The living wands of the Druidic tradition lend themselves very effectively to casting and binding intentions of all kinds, including curses, as their living core not only encapsulates their intrinsic attributes but also works to amplify their inherent potential to a level that is unobtainable via any other magical device. This means that complex curses may be undertaken in the same way as any other intentions, by starting with carefully chosen tree species, enhancing their individual attributes by crafting various combinations of wood types into compound wands, and augmenting them further and fine-tuning them by entwining other influential botanicals around the shaft. In most instances, this unique ability to craft and fine-tune living wands is used to benefit the recipient of the intention, but what follows is a detailed account of how the same techniques and resources may be employed in a much more sinister way.

Wands for Curse Casting

Living curse wands are typically crafted from the wood of either the holly tree or the corkscrew hazel plant. To review our discussion of the corkscrew hazel wand see chapter four, "Wand Types." The following example explores the use of holly to craft a living curse wand, but the process is exactly the same should the adept chose to use corkscrew hazel.

In addition to its more common virtues, holly has the more malevolent attributes of hate, vengeance, ill will, and enmity. For this reason it is often used to craft wands intended to cast curses. When planned to be used in this way it is best harvested at night, ideally in a lightning storm. Harvested in this way the wood is known as *lightning holly*. Lightning wands—wands crafted from branches harvested during lightning storms—are the most potent living wands used for curse casting. The choice of the individual donor holly tree is made with consideration to all the external influences we have seen before. Once harvested the branch is secured in a protective wrapping until it is to be crafted.

Again, when working with wands intended for malevolent use it is more important than ever that all work is undertaken within a sealed and cleansed protective circle, both to prevent unwanted energies intruding into the space and influencing the wand and to prevent the energies of the curse working from escaping before the intention is cast and causing undue negative effect on any external latent energies.

The crafting of a curse wand begins at a working stone arranged with the necessary materials: a harvested holly branch secured in its protective wrapping, a lit ritual candle in a candle holder, a ritual knife, a small ceramic bowl containing either twelve rowan berries or twelve nightshade berries, a mortar and pestle, a jug of moon-cleansed water, a small wooden spoon, and a clean linen cloth. Rowan or nightshade berries are used because of their affinity with dark workings and their attribute of empowering the energy of the curse, while holly brings these attributes together with its own ability to contain the malevolent energies of the curse as it is channeled through its core.

The crafting working begins with removing the holly branch from

Newly harvested holly branch and rowan berries in preparation for the crafting of a living curse wand. (See also color plate 12.)

its protective wrapping. Then all the leaves are removed from the branch's shaft other than the final few at its tip. The heel-end of the branch is cut diagonally to allow it to sit comfortably in the heel of the palm during the casting. All of the removed leaves and wood trimmings are retained to be returned to nature. The berries are tipped into the mortar and ground to a paste using the pestle. The moon-cleansed water is added to the mortar and stirred with a wooden spoon to dilute the paste until it is a free-flowing liquid; the liquid is then poured back into the ceramic bowl. The tip of the wand is placed in the center of the mortar and held with the left hand, while the bowl of berry liquid is raised in the right hand and a little is poured onto the ground as the adept recites the following or a similar self-composed *anointing intention:*

> What comes from nature is shared with nature, with
> gratitude and recognition of the eternal power of the
> natural world.

The berry liquid is then poured along the length of the wand's shaft as it is rotated to ensure that all of the surface is anointed. As this is done, the adept recites:

> The juice of these berries and the potent energies
> contained within them are the gift of nature and by
> anointing this holly wand with their elixir I imbue
> it with the spiritual energies that will empower the
> casting that follows with the hidden and secret forces
> that nature holds within.

Once the entire contents of the bowl have been poured over the wand it is held in place for a few moments to allow the surplus liquid to drain into the mortar. The wand is then held aloft by the adept with one hand at each end. With the wand held high, the adept recites the following (or similar) *potentializing intention:*

> This work elevates this wand beyond the mundane
> and empowers it with the mighty elemental forces
> held deep within our world, raising them from far
> below and drawing them down from the very heart of
> the cosmos.

The length of the shaft of the wand is now passed through the flame of the ritual candle as the adept says:

> Now I seal them within this holly wand where they
> will remain until they are cast forth.

The wand is placed aside on the linen cloth where it is allowed

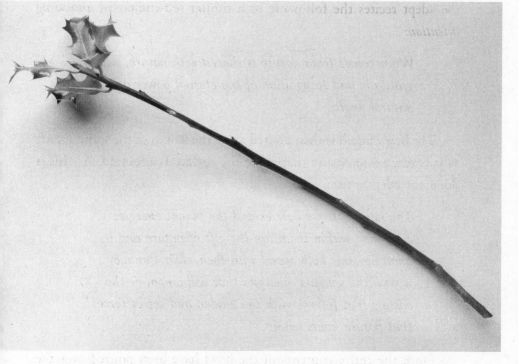

A crafted living curse wand made from holly with leaves at its tip,
ready to be used in a casting.

to dry before being secured once again in its protective wrapping.
In almost all instances, the wand is then immediately used to cast
the curse.

How Curses Are Cast

As with all other intentions, the wording of a curse is composed by
the adept prior to the casting and is usually written on a small piece
of paper or parchment so that it may be attached to the wand after
the casting before the wand is securely stored in a secret place in
case it may be needed to amend or annul the curse at a later date.
The importance of securely storing the wand with the written curse
cannot be over emphasized because, as mentioned, if it is found by a
third party it may be used to release the original recipient from the

curse and bind the same curse to the adept who initially composed and cast it.

In the majority of cases, the potentialized holly wand is used to cast the planned curse immediately after it is crafted and while the protective circle remains sealed. This being the case, to cast the curse the adept stands before the working stone and focuses his mind on the wording of the intention (the curse), firmly locking it in his mind. Then, in a conscious, calm, meditative state, the internal energies are gathered together from the three body centers (the mind, the heart, and the solar plexus), as we have seen before, and focused at the heel of the hand. Facing the intended recipient, whether it is present or the person, object, or place is "beyond the horizon," the adept picks up the curse wand and holds it in the normal wand grasp for basic wands with the diagonally cut heel-end of the wand in firm contact with the adept's palm. The gathered energy held at the interface between the palm and the wand is now amplified by the adept into an energy globe until he feels it cannot be contained any longer. At this moment, the wand is raised and pointed toward the recipient, the gathered energy is released through the core of the wand, and the adept recites the prepared intention as he visualizes the energy globe, wrapped in the spoken intention, coursing through the core of the wand, leaving its tip, and journeying to the recipient where it is absorbed and bound by the words of the adept. With the casting complete, the adept raises the wand high, points it to the sky, and releases himself from the casting meditation in order to return to the mundane.

If the adept is confident that he will never need to amend or annul the curse at any time in the future, then the discharged curse wand is broken in two at its center point and returned to nature. Again, often the wand and the written intention are secured in protective wrapping and carefully stored in a secret place where they cannot be found by anyone else, in case it may be necessary to rework the casting at a later date. This completes the technique for casting the original curse. We may now turn our attention to the subject of casting a counter-curse.

How to Cast a Counter-Curse

Casting a counter-curse may be done in one of two ways: either by a completely new working requiring the crafting of a new living wand or by using the wand used to cast the original curse to then cast the counter-curse. While a working using a new living wand is a powerful casting, it may only be used to lift the original curse from its recipient, whereas if the original wand is used it is possible to not only lift the curse but, if required, to also bind it to the original caster in perpetuity. Again, both workings are dangerous and the consequences of each need to be carefully considered. Lifting or annulling a curse by casting a counter-curse countermands the working of another adept who we must assume had good reason to cast it in the first place, so we must establish the exact reasons for the original casting and the ramifications of lifting the curse and, more extremely, of binding it to the original adept in perpetuity. Having looked at casting a curse with a living wand and the principles that underpin this practice, there should be no doubt remaining as to the risk of this perilous working to both the adept who casts it and the recipient to whom it is bound. An adept should *only* undertake these workings if he is confident that he fully understands the risks involved and is prepared to accept the consequences of his actions.

When an adept becomes aware that a curse has been bound to an individual, object, or location, there are a number of questions that must be asked. Why was the curse cast and bound in the first place? What effects are taking place? Do these effects improve the circumstances or make them worse? Can any other action be used to better effect? If so, what may it be? There are, of course, many other questions that may be asked and these will undoubtedly vary according to the individual circumstances, but the underlying purpose of these questions is to establish whether the existing curse is doing damage and, if it is, then what is the best way to improve the situation. If the adept firmly believes that a counter-curse is needed to annul the original curse then the simplest and most direct intervention is to cast a counter-curse using a new living wand by the means of the working that follows.

Casting with a New Living Wand

As with all curse casting, including the casting of counter-curses, the most frequently used donor species for crafting the requisite wands are either holly or corkscrew hazel. As the working is deliberately intended to be convoluted and secretive, we shall use the corkscrew hazel wand for the following example as its attributes include the ability to confuse and misdirect any scrutiny.

The chosen donor tree and branch are identified using all of the criteria we applied in our earlier examples, taking into account the internal attributes and external influences previously explored in detail. As usual, once the individual branch is harvested it is secured in protective wrapping until it is to be used, which must be as soon as possible if its vital energies are to be retained.

The counter-curse working is undertaken inside a protective circle. The working stone is prepared with a lit ritual candle, a small ceramic

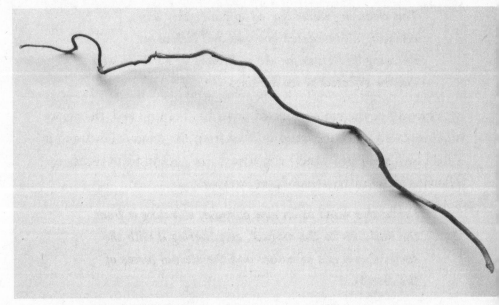

Corkscrew hazel living wand, crafted and ready for use.

bowl, a vessel containing moon-cleansed water, a ritual knife, a clean linen cloth, and the harvested corkscrew hazel branch. The harvested branch is removed from its protective wrapping and any remaining leaves are removed, leaving the surface clean and smooth. The heel-end of the branch is cut diagonally to allow for secure contact with the hand of the adept during casting. All the trimmed leaves and wood are retained to be returned to nature. The vessel of water is lifted high with the right hand and a little of the contents are poured onto the ground as the adept says:

> *What was given by nature is shared with nature, in thanks and recognition of the eternal energies that nature contains.*

Holding the wand in the left hand with its tip inside the ceramic bowl, the moon-cleansed water is slowly poured over the shaft of the wand, making sure all of the surface of the wand is anointed while the adept recites the following or a similar self-composed *intention of purification:*

> *This cleansing water is used to purify this wand, removing all unwanted energies and influences, releasing its virtues for the well-being of all those who may be effected by its workings.*

Once all of the moon-cleansed water has been poured, the empty vessel is placed aside, the wand is lifted from the ceramic bowl, and it is held high with two hands, one at each end, as the adept recites the following (or similar) *potentializing intention:*

> *I raise this wand to its new purpose, elevating it from the mundane to the magical, empowering it with the spiritual energies of nature and the eternal forces of the cosmos.*

Retaining the same grip, the shaft of the wand is passed through the flame of the ritual candle, and as the flame is passed along the wand's length the adept says:

> *I use this flame to seal these spiritual energies within this wand's substance so that it may enhance and magnify my intentions as I channel them through its living, vital core.*

The wand is then wiped clean with the linen cloth and carefully placed at the center front of the working stone. Usually, the casting of the counter-curse is done immediately following this cleansing and elevation, but if there is to be any delay the wand is secured in its protective wrapping until it is to be used, which must, in any case, be as soon as possible.

Typically the counter-curse is composed by the adept beforehand in preparation for the casting and differs from other intentions in a number of ways. In particular, reference is made to the time and date of the initial curse casting, the recipient's location at the time, and the source of the casting (if known). As the results of the curse casting will of course be apparent in some form or another, it will not be too difficult to reconstruct the wording of the curse, or at least a reasonable approximation. This information will be used within the counter-curse to ensure that all the elements are accurately identified along with the intention to be used to nullify it. An example of a potential counter-curse may be:

> *To prevent any further suffering and to nullify any earlier or current hardship, I direct these projected energies upon* [name of recipient], *who was intentionally cursed at* [time of casting] *on* [date of casting], *while dwelling at* [location of recipient at time of casting] *and innocently going about* [his/her] *business with no ill intent or malediction, neither speaking ill of any person nor wishing anyone harm.*

I release [name of recipient] *from this unjustified and unnecessary curse, bound to* [him/her] *without cause or reason, without foundation or justification, but borne through ill will and spite. May this curse be lifted, and its energy be dissipated throughout the cosmos, from this moment forth and forever.*

It is important that as much of the information called for within the brackets as possible is included in the counter-curse. If it is not possible to discover all of the information, then as much as is known may be sufficient, but the more that is stated the better the prospects of success. With the counter-curse composed and the living wand cleansed and potentialized the casting may begin.

Standing within a protective circle, the adept picks up the wand and faces the recipient (or the direction of the recipient if the counter-curse is to be cast beyond the horizon). Before lifting and pointing the wand, the adept gathers his energies from the three body centers and focuses them as an energy sphere at the heel of the hand, as we have seen previously. The counter-curse wording is then repeated mentally by the adept until it is firmly in their mind. Raising the wand and pointing it at the recipient, the adept again repeats the counter-curse mentally as they visualize wrapping it around the energy sphere at the heel of the palm. With the counter-curse in position around the sphere, the adept amplifies the gathered energies at the interface between wand and palm until they can be restrained no longer and then speaks the counter-curse out aloud as they visualize the energy sphere with its counter-curse channeling through the core of the wand, journeying to the recipient, wrapping itself around the person, object, or location and becoming absorbed into their nucleus. At this point, the essential energies that make up the counter-curse envelop the original casting, leave the recipient, and dissipate into the ether. When the recitation is complete, and the adept is confident the counter-curse has been expelled toward the recipient, the wand is raised high and pointed to the sky before the adept returns his focus to the mundane world and relaxes. With the casting of the counter-curse complete, the wand is destroyed by breaking it into four pieces, *all* of which must be retained and returned to nature along with the leaves and offcuts from the earlier crafting. Returning the wand parts to nature is done as soon as possible after the casting. This completes the working for using a newly crafted wand to cast a counter-curse. Next we explore the more dangerous and secret working of casting a counter-curse using the wand that cast the original malevolent curse.

Casting with the Wand that Cast the Original Curse

If the original wand has been retained and stored in the proper way, and if a second adept can gain unfettered access to it, the living wand that cast the original curse may be used to cast a counter-curse in order to unbind the curse from its recipient, redirect it to the individual who first cast the curse, and bind it to them in perpetuity. This practice is seldom used as it can be hazardous in its undertaking, devastating in its outcome, and completely irreversible at any time in the present or the future. The result has a profound effect on two individuals, assuming the recipient is a person and not an object or location. The recipient of the original curse is relieved of its influence and everything that has been affected by the curse is restored. Equally as important, the individual who cast the original curse is subsequently bound by its same influences for eternity. These two outcomes are enacted by the adept who casts the counter-curse and any and all consequences that ensue are his responsibility alone. This being the case, this working cannot be entered into lightly or without serious and detailed consideration. If the proposed working is successful then the original recipient's life will be significantly changed, potentially for the better, while the individual who cast the original curse will have all its difficulties and harm bound to him for eternity, even if he was casting it for a third person who remains outside the influence of the counter-curse.

It can, of course, be argued that the individual who cast the original curse would have been aware of the potential of the intention being reversed when he cast it and that he did so with the knowledge that it could be redirected to himself at any time in the future. But history tells us that very few counter-curses have been cast without attracting the ire of the original adept and that retribution soon follows. Even so, this should not deter the responsible adept from undertaking what his ethics dictate or from putting right what others may have unfairly damaged. Often in these circumstances diligent research reveals what may be right or wrong and the adept's intuition will always play a major role in such demanding decisions.

Gaining access to the wand used for the original curse casting may also further complicate what is already a difficult process. If the discharged curse wand has been stored in a secure, secret place within the individual's workshop or home, then acquiring it in order to bind the curse to the owner and then destroy the wand so it cannot ever be used again will inevitably be difficult. On the very few occasions that I have undertaken this working, the original wand was voluntarily given to me by the adept who originally cast the curse as a result of the overwhelming guilt the person experienced after casting the curse. As it happened, the curses were of no great significance and each adept dealt with the redirection as a matter of course and without undue anxiety, but that is not to say that all counter-curses are as inconsequential, as many are much more complex and have much more profound and intrusive outcomes. On the assumption that, following appropriate research and consideration, the adept has decided that a counter-curse is the preferred action and that the adept has acquired the original wand used in the initial curse casting, we will now explore the working employed to effectively cast a counter-curse using the original curse wand.

The counter-curse is composed beforehand and either written down or set firmly in the memory of the adept who is going to cast it. It must be composed in direct response to the original curse; there is no such thing as a standard counter-curse, and each counter-curse must be destroyed once it has been cast. No counter-curse, or any other composed intention, can be used more than once. The nature of using the wand that cast the original curse to then cast the counter-curse means that a unique type of intention must be composed in order to first lift the curse from the original recipient and then redirect it toward the individual who first cast it. As we will see, the counter-curse working consists of two elements cast immediately following each other. The spoken intention, therefore, is made up of two parts: the first crafted to remove the original curse, the second crafted to redirect the curse to the original caster and bind it to him for eternity. To some extent, this complicates the composition of the counter-curse, but if, as we have seen above, the adept gathers together all the necessary information (or at least as much as he can), then this both simplifies the task and makes it much more effective. The importance of composing the counter-curse carefully and diligently cannot be over emphasized because the redirected curse is permanently bound to the original caster in perpetuity, and it cannot be reversed, corrected, annulled, or amended in any way; the result will be both profound and permanent. It may be useful to examine a hypothetical example in order to further understand the key principles involved.

In our example, at some time in the not too distant past a curse was cast and bound to a person for reasons that appear to be nothing other than malicious intent. Having gathered as much information as is needed and given due consideration to the criteria explaining above, the adept decides that a counter-curse is the best course of action, lifting the original unjustified curse and redirecting and binding it to the original caster, as is the practice in ancient Druidic lore. The name of the person who originally cast the curse is known, as is the name of the recipient, the individual to whom it was cast and bound. The wand used to cast the curse has been obtained by the recipient. As is most often the case, the exact wording of the original curse is not known, but the observable results are that the recipient's physical and mental health has declined, they have become depressed, they confine themselves to their home, and they are unable to be effective in their career. Through discussion with the recipient, it has been established that the curse was cast in retaliation for an unintentional accident some weeks before the casting and that the curse was instituted as a vindictive and malicious action with no justification. In such a circumstance, the curse is to be lifted and redirected through a counter-curse projected through the wand used to cast the original unwarranted curse. This form of working is made up of two elements: first lifting the original curse, then redirecting and binding the curse to the original caster. This is achieved through two parts that make up the counter-curse, cast immediately one after the other. The wording of both parts of the counter-curse must be composed uniquely by the adept who plans to cast it, but may consist of wording such as the following for the *first element of the counter-curse* (to lift the original curse):

> *I use the power vested within this wand, used to cast this unjustified curse, to remove it from* [Name] *to whom it was bound for no warranted reason. I unbind this curse from* [Name] *and return them to full health, lifting the oppressive energies that restrict their activity, depress their mental state, and attack their physical well-being. I remove this malicious intention in its entirety, from every corner of* [Name's] *being and envelop it within this sphere of natural energy until it may be bound to another, worthy recipient. I bring it here, back to the original wand used to cast it, and hold it at its tip with the forces of the world spirit and the eternal energies of the cosmos.*

This first intention is crafted to lift the original curse and return it to the tip of the wand from which it was originally cast, where it is held until the adept enacts the second element of the counter-curse (to redirect and bind the original curse to the original caster):

> *I cast this intention, with all its original meaning and purpose, its ill will and injurious and destructive resolve, toward [Name] and bind it to him in perpetuity, now and forever. May it attract all the adverse energies it was crafted to bind to [Name] only to magnified effect and from this moment forward, bringing upon this person all that it was crafted to deliver only in greater force and with more dire result. With this casting complete, I destroy the wand of casting, dissipate its energies, and remove its influence, ensuring that it will never be used for such malicious purpose again.*

Again, the wording of both elements above is an example only and should not be used unaltered for other castings. It is imperative that each intention is composed by the adept himself in direct response to the circumstances and reflecting his own intuitive response to the situation.

At the core of this counter-curse working is the wand used for the original casting. It is probable that even if the adept is confident that the wand in his possession is the one that cast the original curse, he would be unaware of its treatment between the time when the curse was cast and the time that it came into his possession. This being the case it is imperative that the curse wand be cleansed of any external energies that may have contaminated it while in storage *without* jeopardizing the spiritual connection it still retains with the curse it was used to cast. This is achieved by a working that anoints the curse wand with a purifying potion crafted by macerating freshly harvested botanicals in metheglyn. The various methods of fermenting metheglyn from honey and herbs are explained in a wide range of publications and online resources. The important aspect of the process is to add the various botanicals before the fermentation begins so that they transfer their attributes during the fermentation process, rather than adding them to the finished mead after the fermentation is complete. The libation required for the cleansing will need to be crafted beforehand in preparation for its use in the cleansing working. This may be done at any time as the cleansing potion can be bottled and stored until it is needed. Most often it will be crafted along with other staple libations, ointments, and remedies in the Druid's workshop.

A number of botanicals lend themselves to this *cleansing potion* as they are capable of achieving spiritual purification without inhibiting any latent energies within the device being cleansed. This is an important consideration when the adept wishes to remove intrusive unwanted influences while still retaining the virtues and attributes of the object, person, or place being cleansed. Typically the herbs used for this working are either wild mint, rosemary, or lavender. Each may be used separately or they may be combined in any permutation.

A collection of various cleansing herbs, including rosemary, mint, and lavender, to be used to craft a cleansing potion. (See also color plate 13.)

As with all such preparations, the crafting of the cleansing potion takes place inside a protective circle to ensure its integrity. The working stone is prepared with a lit ritual candle, a mortar and pestle, a vessel of metheglyn, a vessel to contain the macerating liquid, and a clean linen cloth, along with the freshly harvested herb(s).

A small handful of the chosen herbs are placed in the mortar. These could include around three flower heads of lavender, two stalks of mint, or the spiked leaves removed from two six-inch sprigs of

Materials laid out for the crafting of a cleansing potion.
(See also color plate 14.)

rosemary. The herbs are then bruised lightly to release their essential oils and expose their inner energies. The bruised herbs are then pushed into the storage vessel and barely covered with the metheglyn. The bottle or jar is then sealed and placed aside to allow the herbs to macerate for a minimum of seven days, following which it is ready for use.

The *cleansing of the original curse wand* must be completed effectively before the wand may be used to cast the counter-curse. This is done through the following working, which must be done immediately before the counter-curse is cast in order to ensure the integrity of the wand. The working is once again carried out inside a protective circle. Typically the casting of the counter-curse is undertaken from within the same circle immediately after the cleansing. The working stone is prepared with a lit ritual candle, a ceramic goblet, the vessel of cleansing potion, a ceramic bowl, and a clean linen cloth, along with the original curse wand, removed from its protective wrapping. The working begins with a measure of the cleansing potion being poured into the goblet. The adepts sips the potion and then pours a small amount onto the ground while saying:

What comes from nature is shared with nature.

The wand is then raised in the left hand and its tip placed into the ceramic bowl. The cleansing potion is taken in the right hand and slowly poured along the shaft of the wand as it is rotated to ensure all of the surface is wetted with the potion. As this is done, the adept recites the following or a similar self-composed *intention of purification:*

> **I ask that this cleansing potion, imbued with the**
> **purifying spirit of nature, remove all unwanted**
> **energies from this wand that may have inhabited it**
> **since it was last used to cast its owner's intention.**
> **Let these unwanted spiritual forces be removed from**

*this place and returned to the universal energy of the
cosmos in the name of all that have come before me
and all those who will follow.*

When the entire surface of the wand has been anointed and the
last of the cleansing potion has been poured, the adept grips the wand
with two hands, one at each end, and passes the shaft of the wand
through the flame of the ritual candle while saying something like this
potentializing intention:

> *May the spirit of this ritual flame cleanse the body
> and purify the spirit of this wand. May it seal
> its being and prevent any unwanted energy from
> contaminating it. Captured within this wand are
> the residual energies and forces retained from its
> last casting and this ritual flame will revitalize these
> dormant energies and once again make them available
> for my use. May this wand's spirit be reclaimed and
> elevated once more, reconnecting with its earlier
> casting and reuniting me with the recipient and the
> intention bound to* [him or her.]

The linen cloth is then used to wipe the wand clean of any potion
or candle smoke that may be on its surface. It is now ready to be used to
cast the planned counter-curse.

Casting the counter-curse is usually done immediately following
the cleansing, while the adept is still standing inside the protective
circle. First the adept faces the direction of the intended recipient—
the individual, object, or place that was the subject of the original
curse, whether in sight or beyond the horizon. Gripping the wand, the
adept gathers his internal energies from the three body centers as we
have seen before and focuses them at the interface between the wand
and the palm. In silent meditation, the previously composed counter-
curse is recited as it is visualized as being absorbed by the sphere of

internal energy at the interface. Once the counter-curse is absorbed the sphere of energy is further amplified and empowered by the adept to the point where it can no longer be contained. The wand is then pointed directly toward the recipient and the adept begins to recite the first part of the counter-curse as they visualize the counter-curse within the energy sphere being channeled through the vital core of the wand, leaving the tip, and journeying to the recipient where it is absorbed and bound. Following this, the adept visualizes the spiritual energy of the original curse being captured by the same energy ball, emerging from its recipient, and journeying to the tip of the wand where it is held. While still in this meditative state, the adept slowly raises the wand and points it toward the sky while turning to face the source of the original casting. The wand is then lowered and pointed toward the original caster, and while reciting the second part of the counter-curse the adept visualizes the energy sphere, now imbued with the original curse, detaching itself from the wand tip, journeying to the original caster, and being absorbed and bound to him. On completing the casting, the wand is raised high and pointed to the sky. In this position the adept ceases their meditation and returns to the mundane. When he is confident that the working is complete, the adept breaks the wand into at least four pieces and securely stores the discharged pieces until they may be returned to nature.

USING ATTRACTION WANDS, PROTECTIVE WANDS, AND CIRCULATION WANDS

We have seen that the living wands of the Druidic tradition are crafted in a wide range of forms using wood branches selected from a varied collection of tree species. Some may be combined into compound wands while others may be entwined with other botanicals to enhance their attributes. In the majority of cases, the wands we have seen are intended to be used to project the adept's intention, casting it toward the recipient and binding it to them. This group of wands may be classified as *projection wands,* influencing the adept's intention as it is channeled through the wand's core before it is projected from its tip.

Attraction wands are used to channel and influence the adept's intention as he first casts it to the recipient and binds and then uses the wand to attract the recipient back toward the adept or his close vicinity. Typically these wands are hook-shaped, with the straight tip being used for the initial casting (projection) and the hook feature used in a hooking motion to retrieve the projected energies back to the adept. To review our discussion of hook wands, see chapter four, "Wand Types." An attraction working is often compared to catching a fish, where the line, bait, and hook are first cast (the projection), the fish takes the bait (the binding), and the captured fish is retrieved by the fisher (the attraction). Workings using hook wands for attraction may be used to attract romantic emotions, lasting love, well-being, and many other positive influences. Wands other than hook wands may also be used in attraction workings where attraction energy is produced from the composition of the adept's spoken intention, the attributes of the chosen wood species, and any enhancing botanicals that may be entwined around the wand. All wands used in this fashion may be classified as attraction wands, though by far the majority of attraction wands are either hook wands or thorn wands.

Apotropaic wands, or *protective wands,* are used specifically to cast protective intentions, following which they are often also deposited as protective devices once the protective intention has been cast. As we have discussed above, apotropaic wands are crafted from wood species such as rowan, holly, or brambles or from a combination of these woods. They may be entwined with additional protective botanicals to enhance their apotropaic characteristics. Although a protective wand is initially used in the same way as a projection wand—that is, to project the protective intention—after the casting the wand is deposited at the vulnerable place or given to the individual who is to be protected as a form of protective amulet.

Workings with apotropaic wands begin with a protective intention being cast by the adept so that the intrinsic attributes of the wood species being used, along with any additional botanicals, may be absorbed by the projected intention as it is channeled through the living core of the wand. Once the intention has been cast, and it may often be cast in the form of a protective circle or a protective barrier or wall, a further intention is spoken by the adept producing a protective "radiation" that emanates from the protective wand itself. The wand is then deposited at the most vulnerable location in the space to be protected so that it may prevent the intrusion of any unwanted malevolent energies or influences. As we have seen, the same working may be undertaken using apotropaic bundles (page 151). Protective wands and bundles are the only living wands that are not immediately returned to nature once they have been discharged; instead they are left in place to continue their influence in perpetuity.

Circulation wands are another unique variety of device employed solely within the Druidic tradition. Their purpose is to invest the virtues of the chosen wood species into the internal energies of the adept as he meditates or contemplates. Unlike all other living wands, circulation wands affect only the adept's internal energies and are not used to imbue their virtues upon a projected intention. However, they work in the same way as other wands in that the adept's own internal energies are influenced as they are channeled through the living core of the wand.

Because of the nature of circulation wands, the wood species most frequently used in their crafting are oak, for its virtue of wisdom; yew, for its association with divination and the otherworld; rowan, for its attribute of opening portals to the other world; and willow, for its association with travel, water, and contact over long distances. Circulation wands are often crafted as compound wands in order to balance or fine-tune their attributes, with wood species having protective virtues added to safeguard the more subtle virtues of the other woods. In the same way, circulation wands are frequently wrapped with entwining botanicals to influence or protect the principal species' attributes. The main shaft of the wand may be entwined with dog rose, for example, to emphasize any love, mint to purify the intention, or ivy to bind the intention powerfully to the adept's internal energies. The harvesting, crafting, and potentializing of a circulation wand follows the same criteria and methodology as for all other wands. The only difference is that during the crafting, both ends of the wand are cut on the diagonal to expose the wood's inner core and the final two inches of the bark are stripped away at each end, revealing the inner white wood at both ends of the wand. This is done in order to facilitate the secure contact of each end of the wand with each of the adept's hands so that the internal energies may circulate freely through the wand's core.

A living circulation wand crafted from oak wood, showing both tips stripped of bark to enable the correct hand grip and contact.

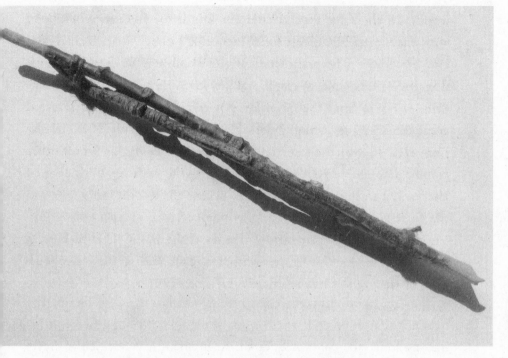

A compound living circulation wand, crafted from oak wood and rowan wood to imbue their complementary attributes to the adept as he or she meditates.

The most frequent workings employing the circulation wand are those of contemplative meditation, through which the adept may be seeking to gain a deeper, more profound understanding of a situation or to deepen his knowledge of a particular esoteric subject. Similarly, circulation wands may be used as a means of visualization or spiritual journey, or simply to intensify the adept's internal energies in a specific way in preparation for a particularly complex or profound working that may follow.

The meditative process using a circulation wand involves the adept visualizing his internal energy circulating around his body to the right hand, passing through the living core of the circulation wand, and reentering his body at the left hand before repeating its circuit again, each time passing through the wand's core. As this circulation happens and the adept's internal energies travel through the wand's core, more and more of the wand's attributes and virtues are absorbed into the adept's own energies and the absorption cycle becomes infinite, limited only by the adept's intuition which tells him when the wand's influences have been entirely discharged.

Such workings begin with the adept, having undergone both physical and spiritual cleansing, seated in a comfortable, relaxed posture, prepared to enter a state of contemplative meditation. The adept then gathers his internal energies from the three body centers in the form of a visualized energy sphere, as we have seen before, and focuses the gathered energies at the heel of the right hand. Taking up the living circulation wand, the adept grips it in both hands so that each of the wand's ends is in direct contact with the heel of each palm, forming a connecting bridge between the two. The energy held at the heel of the right hand is then mentally amplified until it may no longer be contained, at which moment it is released to travel through the wand's living core to the other hand, and from there it continues in a repeating circuit up the left arm to the head, dissipating through the adept's brain and gathering into a sphere once again to journey down the right hand to the heel of the palm, where it continues its journey once again around the circuit. As the energy sphere circulates through the wand's core and around the adept's body it absorbs the attributes of the wand's living core. We can see, then, that there is no projection taking place in the working. All of the adept's internal energies, enhanced by the wand's attributes, remain within his body. When the circulation working is complete, the wand is returned to nature, as with all other living wands. It is most important that discharged circulation wands are disposed of properly because, as a result of the way they function, traces of the adept's energies may be retained within the living core of the wands, giving an unscrupulous third party a precise "fingerprint" of the user's personal energies, which, as we have seen, may be used in inappropriate ways.

SUMMARY

In summary, Druidic living wands must be crafted and used in response to the prevailing circumstances; they function in different ways according to how they are elevated and employed; and they function in sympathy to how each individual adept empowers them with his or her own intuition and personal energies. We have seen that there is a wide variety of living wands, each crafted for specific and unique applications and each used in conjunction with carefully composed intentions and castings. Having been crafted for a specific purpose, Druidic living wands can only be used once before being returned to nature.

Using living wands requires very specific skills and insights and imposes a demanding series of necessary steps including identification, harvesting, crafting, potentializing, casting, and returning wands to nature, along with the need to compose a unique intention for each individual working, no matter how simple or complex the circumstances may be. Using living wands places huge responsibility upon the adept as he or she becomes the sole creator of the wands and the sole practitioner of the complex workings for which they are crafted and used. If things go wrong then the adept is responsible, and conversely when things go well the adept has the joy of working with nature in all its wonders. We have seen in the various examples above that over many millennia living wands have been crafted and developed in response to every possible circumstance, and their ability to influence the intention of the adept is a consequence of the individual attributes and virtues that nature has provided to both the adept and an unrivaled collection of tree and other botanical species with the ability to respond to our every need.

The exploration of living wands in this book gives the reader a broad description of the ways in which wands can be used and aligned with variables such as wood species, wand form, wood combinations, and botanical embellishments. Wands may be refined and fine-tuned meaning that almost every situation, no matter how complex or convoluted, may have an appropriate living wand crafted specifically to respond directly to it.

Next we will explore the way in which we return these gifts to their original source and how we do this without adversely affecting the balance of nature and the abundant materials nature provides.

EIGHT

RETURNING YOUR WAND TO NATURE

Return Ritual

In every case, once a Druidic living wand has been used and the wand has discharged its energies it is carefully stored until it is to be returned to, and thus reunited with, nature. As with every Druidic device derived from the natural world, the material of the device is returned to its original natural environment, ideally at the same location from which it was originally harvested. As well as the device itself, such as a living wand, any botanical adornments, enhancing herbs, or the like as well as any off-cuts or trimmings removed during the wand's crafting are also retained to be returned to their original location.

The protocol of returning all the harvested material to its source location is born from the tenet that the balance of nature must be retained at all times, and that only when botanical material is allowed to decay and reunite with its base matter and spiritual energies, as part of the world reservoir of elemental substance and spirit, may the cosmic balance remain intact, allowing all these precious resources to be used over and over again without depleting or diluting the world's vital reserves.

The process of returning donor material to its source begins during the harvesting, when all of the materials trimmed from the harvested branch such as unwanted twigs, leaves, or sprouting branches are removed from the wand branch, gathered together, and placed at the foot of the donor tree. At the same time, the adept recites words of thanks for the leaves and off-cuts and also for the donated branch, soon to be crafted into the living wand. Similar words of thanks are repeated during the crafting of the wand and as the intention is cast, each in acknowledgement of the gifts of nature and the ways in which the Druid may work with the abundant materials and forces that nature provides, as they are themselves an equal and indivisible component of nature as a whole.

As we have seen, not all living wands are returned to nature immediately after they have been used. Some are retained and carefully stored in case they may be needed to annul or amend the intention they were employed to cast. However, the vast majority of living wands of all types are returned to nature as soon as possible after the casting has taken place and the wand has been discharged. This is achieved by the adept returning to the original donor tree, usually under moonlight, to conduct the return ritual.

The *return ritual* begins with the adept kneeling before the donor tree and assembling the ritual tools. These tools include the discharged living wand, secured in its protective wrapping, a vessel of moon-cleansed water, a ritual knife, and a clean linen cloth.

The first stage of the working sees the adept selecting an appropriate space to deposit the wand. This will be a space beneath the donor tree that allows the adept to clear part of the ground to deposit the wand without destroying or disturbing either the donor tree or any other influential botanicals that may be growing around it. The space will need to be large enough for a small rectangular hole to be dug, approximately a quarter of the wand's length, six times its width, and around six inches deep. Having identified a location, the adept uses the ritual knife to first clear away the surface of any grass or other plants and then digs a rectangular hole as described above. The removed earth must be

Equipment for the return ritual, used to return a living wand to nature.
(See also color plate 15.)

kept close by as it is used to refill the hole and cover the wand after it is deposited. With the hole prepared and the ritual tools arranged around it, the working may begin.

The adept first removes the discharged wand from its protective wrapping; holding the wand in her left hand, she lowers the tip into the hole. Raising the vessel of moon-cleansed water in her right hand, she pours a steady stream of water over the shaft of the wand while slowly rotating it to ensure the entire surface is anointed. As this is done the adept recites the following or a similar self-composed *returning intention:*

> *What is given by nature is returned to nature. I anoint this wand with this purifying water so that it may return to its natural habitat as pure and uncontaminated as when it was donated. May this cleansing water reinvigorate this branch and, by anointing the roots of the donor tree, bind the two once more, making the two into one and restoring the balance of nature as a whole.*

With this, the adept places aside the vessel of water and holds the wand with one hand at each side of the middle of the shaft. Raising the wand high, she snaps it in half at its center line while reciting:

> *No longer a living wand—I break and destroy this wand as it becomes a branch once more. No longer a tool of workings, no longer a channel for good intention, no longer an amplifier of my energies—I relieve this branch of its ritual status.*

Placing the two halves of the branch together and again gripping them with both hands near the middle of the shaft, the adept breaks each of the two pieces in half again while reciting:

> *The wand is destroyed and incapable of further*

use. I thank nature for its gifts and return what
has been loaned. The balance of nature is restored,
and the universal spirit of all things returned to its
equilibrium.

The four pieces of the wand are then placed into the hole and covered with the reserved earth. Once covered, the adept again picks up
the vessel of moon-cleansed water and slowly pours the remaining water
over the earth covering the deposited branch while reciting:

I seal this deposit, reuniting branch and tree in the
eternal cycle of life and death. May no one disturb
this place as nature takes its course. What comes
from nature is returned to nature. The balance is
restored.

This completes the return ritual, and the workspace is disassembled.
The space and area where the wand was returned is then usually tidied
and rearranged so as not to attract unwanted attention, ensuring that
the deposit remains undisturbed.

This same ritual, with the wording of the intentions being composed by the individual adept, is used in returning all forms of living
wands to their original location. It is also used with the wording suit-
ably amended, for most other botanicals or minerals that may have
been harvested for ritual use, which must never be overlooked or forgotten. The return ritual creates the final bonding of the intention(s)
that the wand cast, prevents the same castings from being annulled
or amended, and prevents the discharged wand from being used for
malevolent workings. Most importantly, completing the return ritual
fulfills the adept's continued responsibility to maintain the balance of
nature and respect all its material and spiritual resources. It must not
be forgotten that we are all a part of the same nature, imbued with
its shared material and spiritual essences, and that as adepts we work
within nature, not alongside it.

CONCLUSION

Although the stereotypical image of the Druid depicts him holding a staff, there is no doubt that the living wand is the most potent and most frequently used magical device in the adept's cache. We have seen that Druidic living wands come in many forms, including the staff, but importantly all have a number of unique attributes and virtues that raise them above the wand traditions of other belief systems. It may be that we have become so accustomed to seeing images of witches flying on their brooms, conjurors projecting beams of powerful light from the tips of their decorative wands, and wizards with crystal-topped staffs using them to illuminate forests and caves that it seems easy to forget that flying staffs, wands, and other such devices are an essential part of the magic lore of many of today's living spiritual traditions. But what elevates Druidic living wands of all kinds beyond similar devices used in other systems? The answer can be found in their name: Druidic *living* wands.

Most belief systems that employ wands in their magic select the tree species from which they craft them by choosing a wood that is believed to be imbued with the particular characteristics that will complement the workings or spells the practitioners intend to cast. Many belief systems, as with Druidic lore, draw on the experience of their ancestors

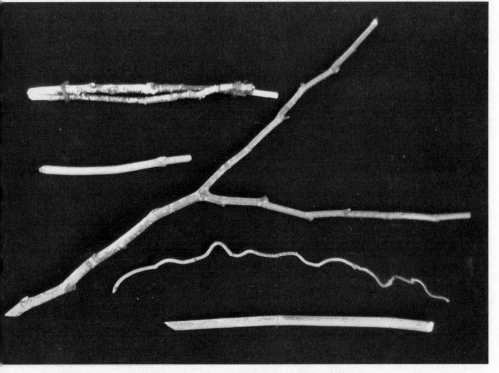

A collection of Druidic living wands, each ready to be used for a casting.

who, through many successive generations, have identified which woods are imbued with particular characteristics, and practitioners draw upon this body of experience and knowledge to identify the tree species of their choice. Some systems believe that the wood species and the wand crafted from it should be matched to the spiritual characteristics of their user, while some believe that the wand's characteristics must be matched to the use it is crafted for.

Whichever characteristics the tree species is selected for, there are diverse opinions on how the appropriate wood should be obtained. Some individuals believe the wood should be cut from a prime, mature example of the species they have chosen, while others believe that only naturally fallen wood should be gathered from the forest floor, where it has been voluntarily shed by the tree as a gift to the finder. Yet others believe that the origin of the wood is immaterial and they are happy to recycle wood previously used for other purposes—upcycling abandoned chairs, tables, and such into magic wands—as long as the wood species is of their choosing. In these latter cases, as with those crafters who buy their wood from timber merchants, there is no importance placed upon the wood's place of origin or the way in which it was felled and cut; the only relevant consideration is the tree's species. It is also apparent that for these practitioners, the age of the wood their wands are crafted from is unimportant, and in all these cases the wood has been dried, aged, and seasoned well before it is turned into a magic wand. It may of course be understandable for some practitioners to believe that as the wood (and the wand) ages, its intrinsic attributes mature and may even become more concentrated, and also that the longer the adept owns and works with the wand the more each bonds with the other as their energies continue to meld over time. There are also practitioners who choose to buy wands from retailers and online sellers, selecting their wands on the basis of the wood species and their aesthetic appeal. These particular individuals are often the victims of mass manufactures who have no interest in the spiritual energies or virtues of the wands they create. There are also many "wandcrafters" who offer bespoke wands crafted in response to their clients' needs; here once again, the client (adept) who purchases these wands is wholly dependent upon the integrity (and ability) of the wandcrafter to craft the wand he seeks. My experience while researching this area is that most wandcrafters are more concerned with the appearance of their finished products rather than their ability to influence the adept's workings. The main concern of those who craft wands by turning them on a lathe or by hand-carving is more often the suitability of the wood species for withstanding turning, carving, and varnishing—to thereby produce an "attractive" wand—with many categorizing wood species by hardness and density values rather than according to their spiritual attributes.

We can see, then, that obtaining a wand can be a complicated task or as simple as choosing one from a regular store or online retailer. But as with most things in life, you get out what you put in, and if you are serious about finding the correct wand for your workings then each of the options and criteria explained in the chapters of this book come in to play.

The main reasons that Druidic living wands are unique among magical devices is that all of the criteria explored in the preceding chapters is taken into consideration during their identification, harvesting, crafting, potentializing, and casting along with their return to nature. In Druidic lore, every tree species and other botanical has associated internal attributes and virtues. In selecting the appropriate species of tree for a wand, these would be the first and arguably most important consideration. Then, when the appropriate species has been selected, an individual donor tree must be found. Any potential donor tree is considered in relation to its surrounding environment and terroir in the belief that the spiritual energy of every individual tree is strongly affected by the external influences of the plants and environment that surround it. In the same way, the energies of each tree are enhanced or decreased by other external influences such as its location, maturity, the season and weather during which it is harvested, the time of day or night it is harvested, and the simple working of the harvesting itself. While external influences are important, there are other indisputable beliefs that do not vary under any circumstances.

The most fundamental of these invariable beliefs is that the essential spiritual energies of the tree (and therefore the branch from which the living wand is crafted) are contained in the vital sap that circulates through the trunk and then to each branch and twig of the tree's extremities, supplying the essential nutrients it needs to survive and flourish. As the adept channels her intention through this vital sap within the living wand, its intrinsic attributes and virtues enhance and amplify the projected energies and augment their effect. This simple, inviolate principle informs the successive two principles unpinning the use of Druidic living wands. The first and most obvious is that the living wand *must* be used as soon as possible after the branch has been harvested and crafted, while the wood's sap remains fresh and vital, as—even after a short period of time has transpired—the sap begins to evaporate and the vital energies it contains start to dissipate. The second is that the living wand *must* be harvested and crafted by the adept who is going to use it, as she and she alone is responsible for all of the workings the wand undergoes and performs from its identification through its return to nature after its energies have been discharged.

The personal crafting of each living wand ensures that the adept is in intimate contact with the wand's vital core, spiritually and physically, during the crafting of the wand, the casting of the intention with the wand, and the returning of the wand to nature. This process ensures that the balance of nature is maintained; during it the cycle of life is completed in a way that may not be done with wands of other traditions.

Bearing all of this in mind, it is difficult to understand how wands crafted anonymously from woods with an unknown provenance or wands made with long-dead wood with no remaining vital sap can work in the same way. Or how a single wand, retained for years and used for working after working, can add anything useful to the adept's workings. Individuals must adhere to the beliefs that resonate with them, however; I do not suggest that Druidic living wands have exclusive priority over the wands of any other tradition, but simply emphasize that within the Druidic tradition it is contradictory to use any wand that is not *living*.

I have repeatedly experienced the satisfaction of seeing the successful outcomes of using living wands myself and I have witnessed many Druidic adepts have equally effective results with their living wand workings. The principle of using living devices for Druidic workings harmonizes with the broader concepts of Druidic lore. The importance of using specific donor woods, chosen for the appropriateness of their inherent attributes and virtues to the circumstances of their use, is as imperative as the principle of returning the discharged wand to nature. If we intend to influence the circumstances of the world in which we live, then it is a simple step to accept that we must use the *living* gifts of nature in order to do so and that these living gifts must be returned to nature with grateful thanks for their loan.

Finally, we have seen that Druidic living wands may be crafted and subtly tuned to respond to virtually any and all circumstances, making them the most versatile and popular magical device available to the Druidic adept. Though not most commonly associated with the Druid, living wands nonetheless play a major part in most Druidic workings and, as each living wand is selected, crafted, potentialized, used, and returned to nature in a unique way, they are another aspect of Druidic lore that separates it from the many other folk traditions and belief systems that may also have originated from the same ancient rural cultures of Northern Europe and the British Isles. The intelligent use of living wands in their various forms and manifestations is an important responsibility of all those who choose to follow the Druidic tradition. Accepting this responsibility both acknowledges the potent energies that govern the world in which we live and respects that the gifts of nature, as part of the greater world spirit, may influence events, places, and individuals in a positive and beneficial way.

INDEX

Page numbers in *italics* refer to illustrations and color plates.

BOOKS OF RELATED INTEREST

Flower Magic of the Druids
How to Craft Potions, Spells, and Enchantments
by Jon G. Hughes

The Druidic Art of Divination
Understanding the Past and Seeing into the Future
by Jon G. Hughes

Witches, Druids, and Sin Eaters
The Common Magic of the Cunning Folk of the Welsh Marches
by Jon G. Hughes with Sophie Gallagher

A Druid's Handbook to the Spiritual Power of Plants
Spagyrics in Magical and Sexual Rituals
by Jon G. Hughes

The Healing Practices of the Knights Templar and Hospitaller
Plants, Charms, and Amulets of the Healers of the Crusades
by Jon G. Hughes

The Ancestral Power of Amulets, Talismans, and Mascots
Folk Magic in Witchcraft and Religion
by Nigel Pennick

Ogam: The Celtic Oracle of the Trees
Understanding, Casting, and Interpreting the
Ancient Druidic Alphabet
by Paul Rhys Mountfort

Secrets of the Druids
From Indo-European Origins to Modern Practices
by Teresa Cross
Foreword by Stephen E. Flowers, Ph.D.

INNER TRADITIONS • BEAR & COMPANY
P.O. Box 388 • Rochester, VT 05767
1-800-246-8648 • www.InnerTraditions.com

Or contact your local bookseller